Philosophy with Teenagers

Also available from Continuum

But Why? – Sara Stanley and Steve Bowkett
Pocket PAL: Creating Enquiring Minds – Sara Stanley
Teaching Thinking, 3rd edition – Robert Fisher
100 + Ideas for Teaching Thinking Skills – Steve Bowkett
Philosophy in Schools – Michael Hand and Carrie Winstanley

Philosophy with Teenagers

Nurturing a moral imagination
for the 21st century

Patricia Hannam and Eugenio Echeverria

network
continuum

Continuum International Publishing Group
Network Continuum
The Tower Building   80 Maiden Lane, Suite 704
11 York Road   New York, NY 10038
London, SE1 7NX

www.networkcontinuum.co.uk
www.continuumbooks.com

© Patricia Hannam and Eugenio Echeverria 2009

British Library Cataloguing-in-Publication Data
A catalogue record for this book is available from the British Library.

ISBN: 9781855394667 (paperback)

Library of Congress Cataloguing-in-Publication Data
Hannam, Patricia.
 Philosophy with teenagers : nurturing a moral imagination for the 21st century / Patricia Hannam and Eugenio Echeverria.
    p. cm.
 Includes bibliographical references.
 ISBN 978-1-85539-466-7 (pbk. : alk. paper) 1. Moral education
(Secondary)–United States. 2. Philosophy–Study and teaching
(Secondary)–United States. 3. Multicultural education–United States.
4. Education and globalization–United States. I. Echeverria, Eugenio.
II. Title.

LC311.H365 2009
370.11'4–dc22

2009008777

Typeset by YHT Ltd, London
Printed and bound in Great Britain by

Contents

How to use this book

This book is divided into three main sections, opening with an insightful foreword by Ann Margaret Sharp highlighting the role of philosophical enquiry in education for a global world. For the past 40 years, Ann has been developing Philosophy for Children (P4C), otherwise known as the 'community of philosophical enquiry', alongside Matthew Lipman at Montclair State University, New Jersey.

Part 1 offers an explanation of the development of the community of philosophical enquiry together with a detailed reflection on the significance of this work to adolescent identity development. This will be of particular interest to those who already have some knowledge of P4C and seek now to develop their understanding. It will also be of interest to those working in higher education, looking for a more detailed account of the process of philosophical enquiry.

Part 2 develops an overview of the experience of young people in the early twenty-first century, living in an increasingly globalized world. This part builds on the first one and relates to contemporary curriculum development. It shows how enabling young people to engage in philosophical enquiry with their peers in community can form the supportive pedagogical framework needed to nourish a moral imagination and equip them with the necessary skills and attitudes for life in the twenty-first century.

However, if you are new to the subject and looking for a practical introduction, you may prefer to look initially at **Part 3** and read about how to embed the community of philosophical enquiry into secondary school life. This third section is a practical development of the theoretical discussions in the first two sections. For example, Chapter 7 considers how the community of philosophical enquiry can contribute to new developments in each subject, and Chapter 8 shows the advantages philosophical enquiry brings to cross-curricular innovations and in stretching the most gifted and talented students. This section includes a chapter on the training needs of those planning to facilitate philosophical enquiry with teenagers.

Throughout the book you will find 'think boxes' designed to help you reflect on the issues raised.

Abbreviations

D.C.S.F.   Department for Children Schools and Families http://www.dcsf. gov.uk. The UK Government department created in 1997 which aims to bring agencies together who work for children and/ or young people. This is all agencies across education, health and social services in England.

DfES   The Department for Education and Skills existed until 1997 and was the national government department for education in England, while other government bodies had responsibilities in Scotland and Wales. This department was previously known as DfEE (Department for Education and Employment), DfE (department for Education) and DfES (Department for Education and Science).

G8   The G8 is not an international organization, nor does it have an administrative headquarters with a permanent secretariat. It is a process that culminates in an annual Summit at which the Heads of State and Government of the member countries hold talks with a view to finding solutions of the main world issues. The main industrialized countries taking part in this process are known as the Group of Eight (G8).

G-20   Is an informal forum of The Group of Twenty (G-20) Finance Ministers and Central Bank Governors and was established in 1999 to bring together systemically important industrialized and developing economies to discuss key issues in the global economy. The inaugural meeting of the G-20 took place in Berlin, in December 1999, hosted by German and Canadian finance ministers. The G-20 was created as a response both to the financial crises of the late 1990s and to a growing recognition that key emerging-market countries were not adequately included in the core of global economic discussion and governance.

GCE   General Certificate of Education, an academic qualification introduced into the UK in 1951. It consists of two levels, the 'A' advanced level normally being taken at the end of 7 years of secondary education at the age of 18. The 'A' level GCE qualification has been used as the entry qualification to university since the 1950s.

GCSE   General Certificate of Secondary Education is an academic qualifica-
             tion usually sat at 16 after 5 years of Secondary Education although
             students of any age can take these qualifications through many school
             institutions in England, Wales and Northern Ireland. It replaced the
             'O' (Ordinary Level) GCE exam which existed from the 1950s to the
             1980s. Students in Gibraltar and the former British Dominion of
             South Africa also use these qualifications. Students generally take
             between 5–12 single subjects. An international version of the award
             the International GCSE (IGCSE) is taken by young people all over the
             world.

IMF   The International Monetary Fund is an organization of 186 countries,
             http://www.imf.org/external/index.htm. It has as its stated aim to
             foster global monetary cooperation, secure financial stability, facilitate
             international trade, promote high employment and sustainable eco-
             nomic growth, and reduce poverty around the world. It is not without
             its critics and some question whether some of the conditions for loans
             actually serve the organization's aims. During the latter part of the
             second millennium there have been calls for reforms of this
             organization.

OFSTED   The UK **Office** for **ST**andards in **Ed**ucation (http://www.ofsted.
             gov.uk/) inspects and regulates care for children and young people, and
             inspects education and training for learners of all ages across the
             United Kingdom.

QCA   The Qualifications and Curriculum Authority (http://www.qca.org.uk/)
             is a public body in England sponsored by the DCSF. This agency aims
             to lead the reform of education and training programmes that equip
             learners, teaching professionals and employers with the skills and
             support they need to meet the demands of the 21st century. It does
             this through for example developing and reviewing the national cur-
             riculum, working with strategic partners to develop educational inno-
             vations and helping to build education and training institutions that
             benefit all learners.

SAPERE   The Society for the Advancement of Philosophical Enquiry and
             Reflection in Education (http://www.sapere.org.uk/) is a UK charity
             which works to advance Philosophy for Children/Communities (P4C)
             and aims to encourage children (or adults) to think critically, caringly,
             creatively and collaboratively. It helps teachers to build a 'community

of enquiry' where participants create and enquire into their own questions, and 'learn how to learn' in the process.

UN   The United Nations (http://www.un.org/en/aboutun/index.shtml) is an international organization founded in 1945 after the Second World War by 51 countries committed to maintaining international peace and security, developing friendly relations among nations and promoting social progress, better living standards and human rights.

UNESCO   The United National Education Scientific and Cultural Organization (http://www.unesco.org/en/education) was founded on 16 November 1945. For this specialized United Nations agency, it is not enough to build classrooms in devastated countries or to publish scientific breakthroughs. The considered view of this organization is that Education, Social and Natural Science, Culture and Communication are the means to build peace in the minds of men and so secure a good future for all peoples.

UNICEF   The United National Children's Fund (http://www.unicef.org) was created by the United Nations General Assembly on 11 December, 1946, to provide emergency food and healthcare to children in countries that had been devastated by World War II. In 1953, UNICEF became a permanent part of the United Nations System, having its Headquarters in New York City UNICEF provides long-term humanitarian and developmental assistance to children and mothers in developing countries.

WTO   The World trade Organization (http://www.wto.org/) deals with the rules of trade at global or near global level. The bulk of the WTO's current work comes from the 1986-94 negotiations called the Uruguay Round and earlier negotiations under the General Agreement on Tariffs and Trade (GATT). The WTO is currently the host to new negotiations, under the 'Doha Development Agenda' launched in 2001.

Foreword

Most young people are brought up with an appalling arrogance through no fault of their own. The education they are receiving has convinced them that their way of life is the only reasonable way of life. And of course they are wrong. Traditional education, rooted in nationalism and a sense of superiority, is producing a generation that has little understanding of globalization and how it affects their lives and their relationships with others. Many (if not most) children are educated in one culture, or one dominant culture, without coming to understand the ideas, customs, mores and beliefs of other cultures. Emphasis is on information and knowledge rather than on understanding and guiding children to come to some insight into their relationships with others around the globe.

As a result, young people often think that they can judge what is good for others who are different from themselves without understanding what those others think is good for themselves. Learning what others think is accessible only through dialogue. One has to spend time with, talk to, and listen attentively to others to understand how *they* see things, what *they* consider valuable and desirable, and *why* they think the way they do. In the absence of hearing how others would tell *their* stories of how they experience the world, and how *they* see *you* with and your culture, it is impossible to understand others.

How can education prepare the next generation to live in a globalized world? How can students learn how to understand the 'the other'?

Charles Sanders Peirce (see for example Colapietro 2006) tells us that the hallmark of good thinking is the willingness and ability to self-correct. But to self-correct we need to do more than rethink economics, politics, military defence and other social institutions. We need to reconstruct education in such a way that we make a shift from knowledge to understanding the main aim of education. Students must learn how to think well – that is critically, creatively and caringly – enquire co-operatively and make better judgements that will bring about the creation of a better globalized world.

The challenges that young people are facing in the early twenty-first century, with all the problems of globalization, oblige society to provide an education that ensures students have the skills and understanding they need to confront these challenges successfully.

This work by Patricia Hannam and Eugenio Echeverria is one of the first attempts to show us how we might use the community of philosophical enquiry to go about this reconstruction of an education that would provide students with the cognitive, social and emotional skills they need to live consciously and actively in a globalized world.

Making better judgements

What is it to make a better judgement in the context of ongoing globalization? How does one go about it? Are there certain things that need to be in place before one can do it? Can I do it alone or do I need others? What is the role of dialogue in such a process? How important is it that I share the perspectives of others – people of different sexes, with different languages, cultures and religions? How important is it that I learn to attend to the details of lives very different from my own? How do I come to understand the plurality of worldviews? Does it matter that I understand what those who are different from me think of as good, important, desirable? Does it matter that I understand what angers, distresses, upsets or hurts them? Moreover, if I am an educator, how do I help my students to go through life in a way that is effective?

Isaiah Berlin (1996) tells us that good judgement is not a body of knowledge that can be taught directly to children or adults, nor is it a scientific discipline with set rules. People who have good judgement do not think in detached, general ways. Their merit is that they grasp the unique combination of salient characteristics that constitute the particular situation. They use powers of close observation to integrate the vast amounts of shifting data that constitute the situation. Such judging requires a direct, almost sensuous contact with relevant data, which are often overlapping and enigmatic. It also requires 'an acute sense of what fits with what, what springs from what, what leads to what . . . what the result is likely to be in a concrete situation of the interplay of human beings and impersonal forces' (Berlin 1996, p. 46). Such a sense is qualitative rather than quantitative, specific rather than general. The ability to make good judgements does not rest on some metaphysical insight but rather on 'ordinary, empirical and quasi-aesthetic experience'.

The ability to make good judgements cannot be taught directly. However, dialogical environments can be created in which children can foster the abilities themselves. A teacher who is well trained in the community of philosophical enquiry can create the conditions in which children can practise the skills involved in the making of such judgements. *Going visiting* is what children do in such a community when they share each other's perspectives and try to build bridges between their different ways of understanding a situation.

Transforming traditional classrooms into communities of enquiry is a slow task involving the immersion of future teachers in such communities. Prospective teachers need to master many skills so that they can model them for their students: building on one another's ideas, offering alternative possibilities of how the world might be, giving counter-examples, detecting assumptions, creating new metaphors, asking for reasons and critically examining the reasons given. Further, it is the teacher who has to model bringing silent participants into the conversation in a non-threatening manner: 'Ana, what do you think of that view?' Sometimes children can easily bridge the various perspectives that arise in communal enquiry, but sometimes they cannot. It is at this point that teachers can help by offering similarities to consider or encouraging the children to think of new metaphors that might take both perspectives into account.

Dialogical enquiry with its distancing, bridging, reasoning, translation, perspective-taking, dialogue and storytelling is essential in learning how to make good judgements. Without it, teachers and their students will never be able to grow in such a way that they discovered themselves making more subtle, caring, informed, wiser judgements in a globalized world.

'Going visiting' in the community of philosophical enquiry

By *going visiting*, Hannah Arendt (see for example 1977 p. 241) means imaginatively entering into the worlds of different people with different views, listening attentively to their stories, trying to figure out the worldviews from which *they* are coming and how they might see you and your perspective as strange. There is a crucial need for students to learn to see such people outside of the culture the students were brought up in, outside of the very assumptions that society took for granted. They have to move imaginatively outside the group in which they feel so much at home. This imaginative travelling causes young people to reconstruct how they understand the world. They begin to see things pluralistically and they discover themselves shifting their priorities, rethinking what is important, adding here, deleting there and slowly creating a different worldview. This activity of moving some things to the background so that one can attend and bringing other things to the forefront so that one can empathize, dropping some details and adding others, imagining how the world looks to the other as well as oneself, is what Nelson Goodman (1978) called *world-making*. It is a continuous work of reconstruction that we undertake because we want to understand the whole.

Having done this, there is more. Children must then *create* – that is, they must tell a story to themselves and others of the *visit to the other culture* in all of its complexity. The broader the range of perspectives the story includes, the more likely it is that the judgement will be informed.

Good, informed judging is possible only within community because it is in community that dialogue and deliberation take place. To judge well is not to arrive at a universal concept but rather to achieve a multi-perspective understanding through communal dialogue, reconstruction, visiting and storytelling – telling oneself the story of the visit, the multi-dimensional perspective that one has entered into, while at the same time remaining oneself and accepting responsibility for the final judgement.

Ultimately, our final judgement is located in our *relationship* to the myriad of views we have taken into account. It is a process that is always dialogical. It is an imaginative and courageous act for children to step back in order to engage in the deliberation that precedes considered judgement. It involves actively trying to remove our own biases and prejudices so that we can listen to others and attempt to understand where they are coming from, what they are assuming, how they see the world. It also involves having the courage to try to bridge the abyss of remoteness so that one can perceive and understand things that at first seem so strange and foreign.

Young people come to realize that behind each different perspective lies a worldview that must be understood *from the inside*. It is not easy but it is possible, especially for children who have not yet dulled their imagining capacities. Such visiting is a huge leap because it affords children the opportunity not only to hear what others think but to receive these different views openly and to consider them seriously for insertion into their own way of understanding the world.

Ways of going visiting

One way to foster this capacity for taking one's imagination visiting is to read good literature – literature that affords children the opportunity to enter into *two* aspects of another's view: the perspective itself as well as the circumstances that give rise to this particular perspective. The contribution that good literature has to make to the formation of future world citizens is its ability to wrest from our frequently obtuse, prejudicial and blunted imaginations an acknowledgement of those who are other than ourselves, both in concrete circumstances and in their thoughts and actions. It is not only having access to different ways of thinking but trying to understand *why* the characters think the way they do. Good novels are works that help us understand how differently people not only think but feel, why they do what they do and what they consider worthwhile. It gives us access to how others perceive the world. Martha Nussbaum (1992) has written extensively of the power of novels to enlarge children's horizons, helping them to see the world from a plurality of perspectives and to cultivate compassion for the oppressed of the world (see also Nussbaum 1995).

Another educational, active and communal way to learn how to *go visiting* is to transform traditional classrooms into communities of enquiry so that children are afforded the necessary conditions to foster the thinking and philosophical imagining essential for understanding people from other cultures and the effect that globalization has on our own daily lives. This can begin early in the life of children, when they begin to acquire language. With language comes the capacity for dialogue with other children, and once one has dialogue one has the tool for going visiting. Such classroom communities foster skills for such visiting: skills of listening, sharing perspectives, empathizing and sympathizing with people from different backgrounds and cultures, while learning how to reason well together in a critical and creative fashion. Such children would soon become aware of the ethical, logical, aesthetic, social and political dimension of their experience and begin to reflect on the democratic procedures that they are using in the classroom, with fairness and goodness as regulative ideals.

The community of enquiry is a safe place where students can 'try on' ideas and have their peers explore with them the implications, assumptions and consequences of such ideas. It is a world where alternative perspectives and alternative values – alternative worlds – can be explored while sensitizing each child to the complexity of the distinctive, different worldviews of each other. It is a caring and imaginative place where one can feel free to tell one's own story, to attend carefully to the unique stories of each other, to learn how to care for people very different from oneself and practise caring about the procedures of respectful, humane, growth-producing communal enquiry.

Further, thinking dialogically cannot rely only on tradition, much less on received ideas or ideology, because changing historical realities have rendered these useless and no longer meaningful. The community of enquiry allows for thinking together as a process of gathering up the fragments of broken traditions and old worldviews and reassembling them anew, imaginatively creating a new worldview that all can share to some degree.

Arendt makes two important distinctions regarding *going visiting*. She points out that it is not meant to suggest touring, nor is it meant to suggest complete assimilation of the perspective of the other. To do either is to erase plurality and difference – essential constituents of good judgement. Tourists, no matter where they go, are detached spectators. For them, it is always a matter of 'me' and 'them'. Often they will go to extremes when travelling to make certain, before they leave home, that they will have all the comforts of home in the foreign place. Deprived of these comforts, they can become quite anxious and difficult (Disch 1994).

Going visiting is also not a task of completely assimilating – that is, 'making yourself at home in a place that is not your home by appropriating its customs. (Disch 1994,). This kind of assimilation involves forgetting oneself and where one came from and doing all one can to become a native of the foreign culture. In order for children to tell themselves the story of an event from an unfamiliar standpoint they have to learn how to position themselves there as themselves, as people who happen to be storytellers. That is, the student can neither stand apart from nor identify completely with the multiplicity of perspectives.

Going visiting is travelling to a new location, leaving behind what is familiar but resisting the temptation to make yourself completely at home in the foreign world. Both the tourist and the one who tries to 'go native' erase plurality.

It's a tricky business, this *going visiting*. Somehow you have to master the art of thinking your own thoughts, but in the place of somebody else, allowing yourself to experience the disorientation and discomfort that is a necessary prerequisite to understanding just how the world looks to someone else and *how you look to that person*. Where traditional philosophers attempted to transcend their own contextual time and place to inhabit the standpoint of 'any' person, *going visiting* is different. It involves being able to imagine how one might feel and think if one were a character in each of the stories shared in a classroom community of enquiry.

Storytelling as a way of understanding

Why do we tell stories? Is it possible that the stories we tell ourselves are the way we make sense of the world we live in? Or to use Dewey's terms, we reconstruct our experience to take in the new understandings we are accruing as we dialogue with people from other cultures. Coming to understand the other is a twofold step: first, children try to distance themselves from the familiar and expose themselves to views and perspectives that are different, unfamiliar, maybe even shocking. The purpose is to try to achieve equality between the self and others by making oneself an 'other' to oneself. Secondly, when one *goes visiting* into the different perspectives, one fosters a practical equality of concern by multiplying the stories in which one imagines oneself to be an actor, always interested in bridging the different stories into a complex and rich tale that does not lose the uniqueness of each of the individual parts. The end product is a work of art; it is good art when it is characterized by unity, balance, complexity and rich texture and is expressive of the plurality of perspectives (Disch 1994, p. 160).

Good storytellers are uniquely suited to do the work of distancing and bridging that is necessary to good critical thinking because their craft demands that they stand simultaneously in a particular location in the world that is, in a sense, next to themselves. It is not generality but the multiplication of particularities that accounts for the possibility of critical understanding.

When one goes visiting one ventures into the foreign world tentatively, sensitively, caringly, attempting to understand the details of that world from the inside and subsequently trying to weave the plurality of perspectives one has gained access to into a story. The story must make sense not just to oneself but to listeners, who are goaded to draw out the meaning for themselves.

Nelson Goodman (1978) stressed the importance of storytelling (whether it is in words or paints or dance or music) as the means human beings have for world-making. The story of each young person in a community of enquiry is a *version* of the dialogue he or she has participated in, a world unto its own, while at the same time overlapping with the stories of every other participant. When students share their stories with each other, it shocks them that there are so many different perspectives on what is important, what is valuable and what is just. How is it possible that we can participate in the same dialogue and yet create so many different *versions*, each of them leading to a fuller understanding of the whole? One child brings a particular perspective to the forefront while another chooses something totally different. One child deletes bits and pieces of the dialogue for coherence, while another adds background information and internal dialogue, weaving the classroom dialogue into a coherent story with multiple characters who manifest inner as well as public lives. One child stresses the emotions of her characters as motivators to action, whereas others focus on how emotions overwhelm characters, depriving them of acting on the world.

Worlds-in-the-making in the community of enquiry

When Goodman (1978) claimed that there are *ways* of world-making he was not denying that we always presuppose some world external to our representation. He was pointing out that there are *versions* of this world that correspond to different ways of description.

When a student offers the group her description of the world, whether it is in dance, paints or words, she is, in a sense, making the world.

For Goodman, there is no one way the world is – there are many versions.

If one listens carefully to the conversation of students as they discuss what it is to be fair or beautiful or true in a particular situation, one realizes that each young person comes to the discussion with her own perspective, which includes her prejudices, misunderstandings and ignorance of the other. These perspectives can overlap in parts, letting the students experience similarities. But the similarities can be few. Children and young people discover a variety of worldviews to the extent that a diversity of cultures prevails in the classroom. Bridging between worldviews becomes the work of the community.

> If I am asked what the way the world is, I must likewise answer, 'none'. For the
> world is many ways. For me, there is no way that is the way the world is; and so of

course no description can capture it. But there are many ways the world is, and every true description captures one of them. (Goodman 1978, p. 31)

Young people in a classroom community of enquiry can come to accept that there is no one single story, no one true account of how the world is and which perspective is the correct one. Attentive listening, dialogue, enquiry and imaginative creativity bring about many *versions* of the world – many coherent understandings of experience. Some of these versions take the form of art, others science. Both are partners in the pursuit of understanding ourselves in relationship to the world.

Evaluating one's story

It does not follow from the above that any story is acceptable. There can be better and worse stories, stories that capture the essence of the dialogue and stories that are completely irrelevant. Young people need criteria to evaluate the stories of their peers. With such criteria, they are not trying to ascertain which story is most true but rather which versions capture a rightness that adds to our understanding of the whole. Goodman suggested the following criteria:

1. How compact, understandable or informative is the story?

2. Does it have more explanatory power than other versions?

3. Does the story render insight?

4. How useful is the story?

5. Is the story plausible?

6. Is the story coherent? Does it contain any contradictions?

When one thinks about Goodman's theory of world-making, one begins to see the dialogical classroom community of enquiry as more akin to an atelier than a room full of desks populated by children waiting to have their heads filled with information. In developing their understanding of the globalized world, students are free to be creative within the bounds of language, logic and what they have come to see as reasonable as a result of the dialogical enquiry with their peers. Their stories are more than a Vygotskyan internalizing of the dialogue in which they have participated. They are creative expressions of how they experienced the dialogical enquiry that they can share with others. In a word, they are works of art. Such storytelling stretches children's imagination to its limits. It forces them to grow beyond their subjective small worlds and enter other worlds, not as another, but as themselves, with insights and understandings that seem to expand with every minute.

Conclusion

There are important connections in *dialogue among students from different cultures*, storytelling, world-making and critical understanding of ourselves in relation to the other. Good storytellers are uniquely suited to do the work of *distancing and bridging* that is necessary. It is not generality but the multiplication of particularities that accounts for the possibility of understanding the world of the other.

Much has been written on the power of narrative to educate children into the awareness of perspectives other than their own, but little has been written on the power of doing philosophy communally and then creating stories to express one's understanding of what action one could take to make the world a better place. Philosophical narratives motivate children not only to think critically, creatively and ethically, but to devise strategies for resisting the destructive aspects of globalization and to create strategies for promoting the constructive aspects of globalization, for example communication and dialogue.

To the extent that the curriculum materials used to foster philosophical dialogue in the modern classroom are models of dialogue and communal enquiry, as well as models of students taking the risk of sharing their views, children are engaged in broadening their understanding of the world that they live in. Storytelling in this sense becomes an essential ingredient of their educational lives.

Good storytellers use their imaginative powers to inhabit a plurality of embedded points of view. They can empathetically enter into other perspectives and then tell themselves the story of the visiting.

This position is not one of cultural relativism. What Hannam and Echeverria are advocating here is a cultural pluralism, the ability to think from a plurality of perspectives and the need to engage with others in dialogue before making sound judgements. This is a complex task for young people but one that they are more than capable of performing if given the right conditions. With the mastery of skills such as imagining, going visiting, world-making and storytelling, coupled with good thinking, comes the discovery of the deep richness of human experience. It could be the case that children and young people are much better at this complex task of creating a complementary version because they are so much closer to the imaginative life.

When children enquire in a community of philosophical enquiry, they begin to realize just how different the world looks from different vantagepoints. Communal enquiry does not assume that consensus is *ultimately* possible. But neither does it rule out the possibility of mutual understanding and some form of cooperation – maybe the creation of new metaphors that we can all live with as we try to solve the problems of globalization.

Patricia Hannam and Eugenio Echeverria have set out to explain, in accessible language based on experience with adolescents and adults in different cultures, what is involved in the educational reform of transforming classrooms in communities of philosophical enquiry. It is not a matter of adding a class here or inserting a new methodology there for a while. Rather, the authors have tried to envisage what would be involved in educational reform that would be suitable for a globalized world. This new vision of education would aim at the transformation of children's understanding coupled with a motivation to act in such a way as to bring about a better globalized world. They have not shied away from discussing curriculum reform, various ways to foster children's imagination and, most importantly, what such an educational reform would mean – how we would have to change our vision radically of how teachers should be prepared. For that they are to be commended. It is hoped that this work will initiate much dialogue in the educational community.

Ann Margaret Sharp
Professor of Education
Montclair State University

Arendt, H. (1958), *The Human Condition*. Chicago, IL: University of Chicago Press.

— (1968), *Men in Dark Times*. New York: Harcourt Brace Jovanovich.

— (1969), *On Violence*. New York: Harcourt Brace Jovanovich.

— (1977), *Between Past and Future*, enlarged edn. New York: Penguin.

— (1978), *The Life of the Mind*, ed. Mary McCarthy. New York: Harcourt Brace Jovanovich.

— (1979), *The Origins of Totalitarianism*, 1 Vol. New York: Harcourt Brace Jovanovich.

— (1982) *Lectures on Kant's Political Philosophy*, ed. Ronald Beiner. Chicago, IL: University of Chicago Press.

Benhabib, S. (1987), 'The Generalized and the Concrete Other', in S. Benhabib and D. Cornell, *Feminism as Critique*, Minneapolis, MN: University of Minnesota Press.

— (1992), *Situating the Self*. New York, Routledge.

Benjamin, Walter (1969), *Illuminations*, ed. Hannah Arendt, trans. Harry Zohn. New York: Shocken Books.

Berlin, Isaiah (1996), 'On Good Political Judgment', *New York Review of Books*, 43.15 (3 October).

Colapietro, V.M. (2006), 'Toward a Pragmatic Conception of Practical Identity', *Transactions of the Charles S. Pierce Society*, 41.2 (spring): 173–205.

Deutsch, Eliot (1992), *Creative Being: The Crafting of Person and Global Philosophy*. Manoa: University of Hawaii Press, HI (2nd edn 2000).

Disch, Lisa Jane (1994), *Hannah Arendt and the Limits of Philosophy*. Ithaca, NY: Cornell University Press.

Elgin, Catherine (1999), *Considered Judgment*. Princeton, NJ: Princeton University Press.

— (1998), *The Philosophy of Nelson Goodman*. New York and London: Garland.

Goodman, Nelson (1978), *Ways of World-Making*. Indianapolis, IW: Hackett.

Levinson, Natasha (2001), 'The Paradox of Natality: Touching in the Midst of Belatedness', in Gordon Mordechai (ed.) *Hannah Arendt and Education: Renewing our Common World*. Boulder, CO: Westview Press.

Nussbaum, Martha (1992), *Love's Knowledge*. Cambridge, MA: Oxford University Press.

— (1995), *Poetic Justice: The Literary Imagination and Public Life*. Boston, MA: Beacon Press.

Smith, Stacey (2001) 'Education for Judgment: An Arendtian Oxymoron?', in Gordon Mordechai (ed), *Hannah Arendt and Education: Renewing our Common World*. Boulder, CO: Westview Press.

Young-Bruehl, Elizabeth (1994), *Global Cultures: A Transnational Short Fiction Reader*. New Haven, CT: Wesleyan University Press.

— (2004), *Hannah Arendt: For Love of the World*, 2nd edn. New Haven, CT: Yale University Press.

— (2006), *Why Arendt Matters*. New Haven, CT: Yale University Press.

Introduction

This book arose from a concern that much of the practical work currently going on in our schools and classrooms is not adequately addressing the task of preparing young people for the grave uncertainties of the coming decades.

The global climate is changing and the precise social, environmental and economic consequences of this over the next 20 years are far from certain. In the years to come a generation of people will be needed who can think clearly, critically, imaginatively and morally about the problems that face us. It seems unlikely that there will be fixed solutions that can be rolled out across the planet. Each place, each community, will face different dilemmas and different practical problems.

More than ever before, young people are aware of what is happening in their world. More than ever before, young people in Britain and elsewhere in Western Europe and North America are in a position to act in a way that could make a difference. However, in reality most people do not act in this way. Why? What is it about several decades of environmental and now citizenship education that has not prevented or ameliorated the present situation?

The increasing mobility of people across the globe and the mobility of ideas through the internet have been accompanied by increased awareness of the plurality of ways of being in the world. Young people will be aware of the differences that come as a consequence of different views on upbringing and differences that have occurred as a consequence of global injustice. Being alongside young people as they make their way through these different perceptions and supporting them as they make judgements regarding acceptable and unacceptable difference is an important role for educators at this time. Working together in the community of philosophical enquiry can be a positive way for young people to gain confidence in themselves and in their capacity to make moral choices on these matters despite the ambiguity of the truth of the different possibilities.

As authors of this book, a range of experiences brought us together, including a shared interest in philosophical enquiry. Our experience of working in different continents led us to a shared view that facilitating young people to think together in guided philosophical conversations can develop the shared understandings our global communities need, and will nurture personal qualities that may help to ensure a positive future for all. This way of working engages what many have called 'higher-order thinking', bringing together many different skills and capacities in a way that connects ideas together in a moral frame, facilitating serious thinking, imagining and envisioning about the future in ways that can lead to empowerment and action.

Working together on the International Youth Congress in Mexico, we have observed in a very practical way just how significant young people find investigating, with their peers, questions of common concern. We have seen how having the opportunity to explore new possibilities, to consider detailed implications and consequences can contribute to increased motivation and purpose as young people make reflected but confident choices about their lives, even in the face of uncertainty.

Inviting young people to engage in philosophical investigations through, for example, 'the community of philosophical enquiry' as envisaged by Matthew Lipman and Ann Sharp, has been shown repeatedly to enable young people to transform silence into action. In this book we consider this process in the light of the present global situation. We look at what will be required of education for the present generation. We look at how the young person needs to grow, supported by this process, from child into morally capable adult. We consider the skills, attitudes and other 'qualifications' needed for a secure future. We do this by considering the global social climate into which the present generation is growing, and we present an educational proposal that can help young people consider moral, cultural and political frameworks for living well together.

In this book we propose, then, an educational model that not only invites young people to find out what is happening in their communities, their countries, their world, but also empowers them to act in ways that could make a difference and to work confidently with others to ensure a just and secure future for all.

Patricia Hannam
Eugenio Echeverria
Chiapas, Mexico.
January 2009.

Part 1

The Community of Philosophical Enquiry

Background and history of the community of philosophical enquiry

1

The 'community of philosophical enquiry' in the form of 'philosophy for children' (P4C) was conceived and developed by Matthew Lipman in the 1960s and developed further at the Institute for the Advancement of Philosophy for Children (IAPC). It is a pedagogical proposal – a pedagogical model – and is recognized worldwide within a framework of many different programmes for teaching thinking skills. Philosophy for children, however, is more than just a thinking-skills programme; it also makes a proposal about the kind of society that is desirable and about the kind of people we should be forming through the educational system, based on values associated with the concept of democracy.

When Matthew Lipman was Professor of Philosophy at Columbia University, New York, in the 1960s, he realized that young people were frequently and often justifiably uncomfortable with some of the features of the society in which they were living. He found some of their concerns very reasonable but he also realized that they lacked the necessary skills to construct sound arguments to fight for what they thought was right. It was then that he formed the view that developing a capacity for good reasoning should constitute one of the basic goals of education and that the necessary tools for this could and should be acquired in elementary school. From his experience of working with undergraduates he concluded that if the acquisition of these skills was delayed until young people reached university level it might already be too late. With this in mind he left his Chair at Columbia and went to Montclair State University, New Jersey, where he founded the IAPC. The Institute was officially recognized by Montclair State University in 1973. At this point others gradually began to collaborate with Matthew Lipman, including Ann Sharp, who began working at the IAPC in 1975.

Over the next decade Lipman developed materials – now published by the IAPC (see Links to Other Organizations) – for promoting discussion in what he called a 'community of philosophical enquiry'. These materials are in the form of novels directed at children. The characters in the novels are supposed to be similar to the children reading them. The difference with average real children is that the children in the novels are involved in experiences and situations where they bring up philosophical problems and questions for discussion. Almost every page of each of them has an incident where children talk about school, norms, freedom, justice, responsibility, or other issues related to these, but always within the context of their own everyday experiences. Each of the novels has a teacher's manual with hundreds of exercises whose main purpose is to help students explore philosophical concepts and ideas within the framework of a community of enquiry.

Although there had been an awareness of P4C in the UK during the 1980s, it was introduced in a more organized way in the early 1990s following the broadcast by the BBC of the programme *Socrates for Six Year Olds*. In this programme viewers were introduced to the work of Matthew Lipman and his novels. Perhaps what really captured the imagination of those who watched this was the broader social vision for education that Lipman was speaking of in that television programme, which now seems to have been prophetic.

In the early 1990s the National Curriculum was being rolled out across England and Wales. Teachers were under pressure. Roger Sutcliffe, Chris Rowley and Karin Murris, among others, had travelled to Montclair State University in New Jersey to work with Matthew Lipman and returned to form what is now known as the Society for the Advancement of Philosophical Enquiry and Reflection in Education (SAPERE). They knew that there had to be a creative way to bring this work to the attention of British teachers without involving a great deal of prescription – teachers in the UK were not going to welcome another set of box files and folders with detailed instructions of what to and what not to do. Philosophy for children was introduced into the UK at this point very much as a thinking-skills *process* that could transform teaching and learning in a very specific and moral way. It was a process that could enhance educational environments supporting democratic education by building a capacity for clear thinking. It was an educational model that valued and nurtured thinking for oneself in relation to others and regarded this as an essential educational outcome for life in a democratic society. A system of training was developed and the work began to grow.

The community of philosophical enquiry

By far the greatest contribution that Matthew Lipman has made to education is the work that he undertook on the development of the community of philosophical enquiry. The vision for this community is that it constitutes a pedagogical space where children and adolescents can share their thoughts and ideas, engaging in discussions where they practise and develop critical thinking. In this space they are helped to construct, define and clarify concepts by exploring issues that have to do with values, developing their moral imagination at the same time.

In the UK we have become familiar with an approach that involves the presentation of a stimulus which encourages young people to develop philosophical questions. This could be a story, a movie clip, a scientific experiment or an event in the school – anything, in fact, which causes some reflection and raises questions. Once the questions are framed the group selects a question using a democratic voting process, and the group forms a circle to explore the question in depth guided by the teacher/facilitator. The role of the teacher changes at this point and she/he becomes a guide for the philosophical enquiry, prompting the students to push deeper by careful use of follow-up questions. This process is explored in more detail in the third part of this book.

When forming a community of philosophical enquiry, it is important to bear in mind the following ten vital characteristics:

- safe environment
- expressing disagreement
- cooperative endeavour
- practice and development of thinking skills
- topics for discussion are based on student interest
- topics discussed are philosophical
- knowledge is understood as evolving constantly
- knowledge is co-constructed
- teacher and students are co-enquirers in the search for meaning
- a space for the development of a personal and social project.

Safe environment

The environment must be safe in all respects. Students must know that in a community of enquiry they can express their thoughts and ideas without fear of others making fun of them or ridiculing what they say. This is because the rules of the interaction in the community are established beforehand with the intervention of the teacher and also the students involved. One of those rules is respect for what others have to say and listening with care and attention. This means not only listening to what they say but trying to understand it and to see how it sits with their own way of thinking about the issue being discussed.

Expressing disagreement

In a community of philosophical enquiry it is acceptable to disagree with what others are saying. At the beginning of work with students you can sense some kind of reluctance to express disagreement. They are used to engaging in discussions in which one tries to win over the other, or to demolish their arguments to prove superiority. This is definitely not the case here. Disagreement is seen as an opportunity to grow. There are two things that can happen when someone disagrees with me – and both are good. The first forces me to look for better arguments to defend what I said, and if I manage to do it my point of view will have been strengthened because my arguments also would be stronger. The second thing that can happen is that despite my best efforts to refute the criticisms that were made of my idea, I am not successful in finding better ways to maintain it. This is also good because it forces me to revise, transform and enrich my way of thinking. All of this is as a consequence of the interactions with my peers, discussing matters that are important to us. When others disagree with what I think and say, and they express disagreement, they cause what Piaget calls cognitive disequilibrium. According to Piaget, there cannot be cognitive growth without cognitive disequilibrium.

Cooperative endeavour

In the community of philosophical enquiry the purpose is to construct knowledge together. This means that it is not a competition about who is the best at constructing arguments to defend their views. The work with philosophical dialogue aims to promote cooperation in illuminating a path to come closer to the truth of things. It is a cooperative endeavour, not an individualistic one. The purpose is growth in common understanding. There is space in the discussions in the community of enquiry for playful testing of each other's ideas, of trying to develop strong claims to back up our assertions, but always within the spirit of respect, tolerance and understanding of each other.

Practice and development of thinking skills

In the community of philosophical enquiry there is a gradual development of thinking and reasoning skills. When they engage in dialogue about a question or concern that they have chosen, students offer examples and give reasons to support their views, analysing alternatives, examining differences of context, detecting underlying assumptions, thinking hypothetically, predicting consequences and relating their thoughts and ideas to those of their peers. Constant practice of these thinking skills in the community of philosophical enquiry does not happen in a mechanical way and it does not happen in a vacuum. Many programmes purport to help students to enhance their thinking by getting them to practise a number of thinking skills. However, most such programmes do this without a specific context that is relevant to the students. An extreme example of this could be something like: 'Monday we do deductive reasoning, Tuesday we work with hypotheses, Wednesday we do problem-solving …' From the perspective of P4C, such programmes do not go far enough in getting students to be genuinely critical, reflective thinkers. The big difference with the community of philosophical enquiry is that the topics around which the thinking skills are practised and developed are topics important to the experience of the students. Some of the processes for developing the thinking skills may be similar, but the distinctive element of P4C is that the content and the context around which those skills develop is relevant to – and comes out of – the daily lived experience of the young people themselves.

Topics for discussion are based on student interest

For this reason, in the community of philosophical enquiry the topics discussed are those chosen by the students on the basis of a stimulus that is provided for them to reflect upon. This can be a piece of literature, a newspaper clipping, a short video, or anything that stimulates their thinking and that they can relate to their own significant life experiences. The fact that the topics are chosen by the students and then related to their own experiences means that there is interest on their part for engaging in this endeavour. This is one of the features that writers in the field of learning and meaning-making, such as David P. Ausubel, regard as essential for effective learning to take place. Ausubel suggests that for pieces of knowledge that society regards as meaningful or important actually to become meaningful for and then retained by the student, there has to be a meaningful connection built by learners between the knowledge and themselves. Ausubel suggests that effective educational environments must construct 'meaningful learning experiences'. This is precisely the environment that is built by the community of philosophical enquiry by enabling the topics of exploration to be founded on the experiences of the young people themselves.

The topics discussed are philosophical

One of the most challenging skills the teacher needs to develop to be able to conduct a community of philosophical enquiry is to turn topics that are not obviously philosophical into a mode of discussion that is itself philosophical. A topic that is philosophical is open to question, controversial, difficult to understand; there is more than one way of approaching it, and it is important for all human beings, regardless of their age or often even their period in history. Examples of philosophical topics are those that have to do with freedom, justice, responsibility, rules, friendship, death, authority, reality, identity, love and many others. When working with adolescents the philosophical concepts will be those that relate to their own experience. One possible approach in an enquiry is, after choosing a question for exploration, to invite the students to relate it to their own experience. Examples of this might be when they discuss their responsibility to take care of the planet, or the choices they make in terms of obeying a rule they feel is unjust, or about leaving school and finding a job, getting married or not, stealing their parents' car to go joy-riding, having unprotected sex, doing drugs, getting drunk, thinking about what they could do to achieve peace in the world – thinking globally and acting locally with regard to so many issues that concern them and about which they feel powerless to do anything.

Knowledge is understood as evolving constantly

Knowledge in the community of philosophical enquiry is understood as dynamic, not static – as ever-changing with the development of new findings in every discipline, encompassing many areas for which human beings have not found ready-made answers. In other words, the understanding of knowledge in the community of philosophical enquiry is that truth itself is not necessarily fixed and external to ourselves as suggested, for example, by the cave analogy of Plato and which comes to us today in the popular perception on the certainty of evidence-based science. Rather, in the work of Matthew Lipman and those following him, there was an emphasis on the work of the American pragmatists such as John Dewey. Dewey suggests that knowledge is found through our experience; he suggests that it is through investigation and questioning that we may find some sense of the complexity of truth. However, the pragmatists go on to suggest that we can never know for sure that there are no undoubtable truths for we can never know what the future will bring. In recent times writers in the world of philosophy for children have been developing these understandings of the problems of truth further through, for example, work with twentieth-century philosophers such as Hannah Arendt, Jacques Derrida and Martin Buber.

Knowledge is co-constructed

The notion of truth in the community of philosophical enquiry is consistent with the idea of the construction of knowledge as being something collaborative and social. Dogmatism and relativism are two extremes considered undesirable within the work in a community of philosophical enquiry. Knowledge can therefore be understood as neither objective nor subjective but intersubjective. This search for knowledge happens within the framework of the values of democracy as understood by Dewey.

The role that knowledge plays in the community of philosophical enquiry is very important and it is vital that its importance is understood and appreciated by the teacher facilitating the enquiry. In this way the teacher/facilitator can facilitate the enquiry to encourage and motivate students constantly to keep searching, to try to find out possible answers for the questions addressed. This comes from a philosophical understanding of education that suggests that the most important gains that come to us through working in dialogical contexts with young people are those in the area of the search for meaning itself. Here in the community of philosophical enquiry we can offer a place where young people can dismantle their existing understandings for a moment. They can then reconstruct new ways of understanding in the light of their own experiences and those of others, with the support of interaction with their peers. Answers are seen as temporary places for resting and gaining more strength to continue the journey of finding out. Answers found in the community of philosophical enquiry can never be seen as the end of the path. There is always the need to look for better answers that could give a new direction to the enquiry or new energy to pursuing further understanding in the same direction.

Teacher and students are co-enquirers in the search for meaning

In the community of philosophical enquiry the teacher and the students are co-enquirers in the search for meaning and the understanding of truth. There might be areas where the teacher has more experience, but overall the questions raised in the community of philosophical enquiry lend themselves to sharing a deepening understanding of the concepts involved. They help teachers and students alike to see that adults do not have all the answers and even that some students could have a better grasp of some of the issues discussed than the teacher. The view here is that if there is truth it needs to come from a moral basis drawn from shared experience.

A space for the development of a personal and social project

Students in a community of enquiry gradually explore questions about the kind of people they want to become and the kind of society they want to live in. Within the space of the community they begin to identify their goals and explore identity issues and practical ways to guide their behaviour towards achieving their goals. In the context of this book this particular element of the community of philosophical enquiry becomes one of the most significant.

When we take these ten characteristics of the community of enquiry into account we begin to build a philosophical understanding of the purpose of education itself within the context of our society. Education cannot exist within a vacuum; we suggest that by working with these essential elements of the community of philosophical enquiry we can understand education as something that advances the participation of its citizens within a social democratic context. Lipman himself became increasingly aware that that there is a set of core values that can be promoted by the community of philosophical enquiry. This set of values has to do with a concept of democracy, especially as understood by Dewey in, for example, his books *Democracy and Education* and *Individualism Old and New*.

This will mean, among other things, that all students in a community of philosophical enquiry have the same right to express their thoughts and feelings knowing that their classmates will listen to them with respect. To support this, the teacher needs to ensure that the different voices of the community are heard and that disagreements are expressed in a reasonable manner, not as attacks or insults toward the student with whom others are disagreeing.

It also means that, when needed, the majority vote has to be respected in making decisions that affect the whole group. However, minority rights are equally important and this means that when majority vote and minority rights are in conflict, reasoning and dialogue will be the means for addressing and trying to resolve the conflict. In the community of philosophical enquiry conflict and disagreement are welcome. They motivate students to find better arguments to defend their positions, to be eager to listen to others who do not think like them and to reach compromises where everyone involved wins. This could mean that both sides in an argument might have to sacrifice some of their original claims in order to reach a third position where everyone involved is satisfied. In such a way the knowledge of the group is co-constructed; shared understanding can develop about the profound and complex way in which nature and the universe are formed. It enables young people to begin to push their understanding of the nature of reality, of the possibilities that they have for determining the way in which they want to live their lives. In so doing they will become active, fully responsible moral agents in their own lives, and less and less open to manipulation by the media and other social forces that seek to nourish conformity and compliance with the kinds of global influences that are discussed further in the second section of this book.

In our regular classrooms work with the community of philosophical enquiry also means fully acknowledging equality between boys and girls of all backgrounds. It promotes the idea of equal rights, of opportunity and decision-making regardless of gender, race, religion or social class.

The development of higher-order thinking in the community of philosophical enquiry

The actions of the facilitator in the community of philosophical enquiry are in reality geared to the development of higher-order thinking. Within the context of philosophy for children, the development of higher-order thinking is understood to take place through an interaction between four key elements: critical thinking, creative thinking, collaborative thinking and caring thinking. The facilitation of these aspects of thinking is discussed in more detail towards the end of Chapter 5.

Critical thinking

The main features of critical thinking are that it is sensitive to context, relies on criteria and is self-corrective.

Being sensitive to context means that critical thinkers analyse the specific features of a situation or context and, after careful reflection, make up their minds about the best course of action to take given those specific circumstances. It also means that a specific course of action that might be suitable in one situation might not be correct for a different one. The critical thinker knows how to discriminate and make good judgements with regard to a variety of situations and contexts.

In the community of philosophical enquiry adolescents put hypothetical situations to the test and talk about alternatives and possible consequences of engaging in them. With the help of their peers, they examine situations that they might confront later in real life, being better equipped to deal with them. Examples of these situations could be taking or not taking drugs, having or not having unprotected sex, abandoning school, or taking their father's car for a joy-ride.

Critical thinking relies on criteria because whenever we engage in it we can give good reasons for what we said or did. So if the facilitator is asked for the reasons for doing something, an answer such as 'because I felt like it' is not an example of critical thinking. This means that engaging in critical thinking requires reflection and analysis of the situation before acting upon it.

Another characteristic of critical thinking is that it is self-corrective because, in a community of philosophical enquiry, from the students' point of view, their ideas and ways of looking at a variety of issues are put to the test. It is a safe place where their peers listen to what they have to say, so young people can express what they really think and try to find reasons to justify it.

However, the fact that the community of philosophical enquiry is a safe place does not mean that there should not be a place for disagreements. People might criticize a way of looking at some of the issues that come up for discussion. This criticism will allow the young person who offers this view into the community to self correct and to grow cognitively and also emotionally. When cognitive disequilibrium takes place there is a need for assimilation and accommodation. An exploration of this will ultimately result in a better way of explaining and justifying their ideas. As a young person working in the north of England over some years with this process said:

> If someone does not agree with me, it forces me to find better ways of defending what I say; to find better arguments to support my claims. And if I am not able to do this, it will force me to revise my ideas and the arguments that supported them, and to transform them into other arguments that are stronger.

Critical thinking is preoccupied with the correctness of thought. Formal logic is a good ally of the critical thinker. There is a concern with building good arguments to support our ideas, to make good inferences and to reach conclusions from well-organized premises. Critical thinking is *rational*, well organized and well structured.

Creative thinking

Another dimension of higher-order thinking is creative thinking. Creative thinking is self-transcendent. This means that the creative thinker always tries to go beyond what is already there – beyond what he or she has done before. The worst thing that can happen to a musician, a poet, a sculptor or a painter is to realize that they are repeating themselves and the artist is therefore the best example of a creative thinker. Creative thinking enhances the capacity of students to make aesthetic judgements, and this is an area that has been very poorly developed in schools. These kinds of judgements about what is ugly and what is beautiful, and sensibility towards the appreciation of art and the creations of humanity, have endured across centuries.

Creative thinking places a lot of importance on the work of the emotions and the imagination. For example, creative thinking is playful and gives the opportunity to create hypotheses such as 'What would happen if ... ?' or 'If I do this, then these could be the consequences ...'

So besides being a priority for the artist, creative thinking also plays an important role in ethical thinking and in reflection on and development of values in children and adolescents. By allowing them to explore a variety of possible situations from their own experience, and exploring the possibilities of a variety of ways to go about them, they gain practice in thinking ahead of things and taking everything into account before making decisions.

The role of intuition, passion and fantasy is also very important for the creative thinker. In the community of philosophical enquiry there will be students who are more rational and well organized in their reasoning. They may be more critical than creative. And there will be others who are more emotional – they follow hunches, they trust their instinct when making decisions, they are more creative. Through work in the community of philosophical enquiry we do not try to give more or less importance to creative or critical thinking, but we aim for an equilibrium between the rational and the emotional. We want students who are reasonable. And being reasonable means taking into account the rational and the emotional when making decisions. Lipman said many years ago that we need to make emotions more intelligent and reason more emotional. Reason cannot be separated from emotion and good decisions always have an element of both. Kant's demand that moral reasoning be purified of emotion is, in fact, 'moral incompetence' (Fesmire 2003). Fesmire develops this further in his book on Dewey and the moral imagination, where he argues that as it is true that conduct may be warped by emotional biases; it is also true that conduct will be warped by absence of emotion. This does not mean that the aim of the work in the community of inquiry is to create a perfect balance between these two aspects of higher-order thinking. What it means is that in any important kind of judgement that adolescents engage in there should be an ingredient of critical but also creative thinking within the framework of values of the community of philosophical enquiry.

Caring thinking

This framework of values is best represented by the third kind of thinking, which we call caring thinking. Caring thinking means that each of the members of the community of philosophical enquiry is concerned for the growth of the others in the community. It also means that we listen carefully; we respect and are accepting of other people's ideas even if they are different from our own. This does not mean that we have to agree with their ideas. It requires a capacity for empathy: to be able to put ourselves in the place of the other. It needs us to be able to imagine how we would feel if we were that other person saying or doing something; to stand alongside the other person and appreciate a shared humanity while acknowledging the reality of the differences between us.

The concept of democracy lies at the core of caring thinking. This has many implications at different levels. In the community of philosophical enquiry it means that each of its members has the same right to participate and to agree or disagree with what is being said. When a decision that affects the whole community needs to be taken, the majority vote is respected but minority rights are also taken into consideration. When a minority is affected in its rights, conflict usually ensues. The community of enquiry is not afraid of disagreement and conflict. It welcomes conflict as an opportunity for reasonable dialogue to begin. Ideally the result of the dialogue will be a compromise in which both parties sacrifice part of their original position, reaching a third one that is satisfying for everyone involved.

The democratic spirit of the community of philosophical enquiry is based to a large extent on Dewey's ideas about participatory democracy. The implications for dialogue in the classroom have to do with its purpose. When there is a conflict in the classroom we use dialogue not to see which of the parties wins but genuinely to put our best effort into solving it and at the same time to grow as a community.

It also means that each member of the community should be concerned for the welfare of the others. It is very telling when you see a child or adolescent in a classroom asking another classmate for his or her point of view 'because most of us said what we thought about it and I would like to know what you think'.

In the community of philosophical enquiry, as it becomes more mature and experienced, the students will begin to take more ownership of the well-being of the enquiry space. All members are accepted as they are, and a concern for the growth and well-being of everyone in the group starts to develop. This can be exemplified in this account of one teacher who, while working with a group of adolescents in Nebraska, tells how one student always wanted to express his opinion and his hand was raised most of the time. It would have been easy to allow this student to contribute almost constantly to the enquiry because he was also very coherent and contributed constructively to the advancement of the discussion. The facilitator of these enquiries recalls:

> I was aware that other members of the group seldom participated. I thought they felt a little threatened, feeling that what they had to offer to the group would not be as good. I spoke with Trevor and asked him to help me see what others had to say about the topics for discussion. Since then he became aware and interested not just in his own point of view but also in what his classmates had to offer. He became a kind of ally and in a way learned some of the skills for conducting a community of philosophical enquiry by engaging his peers. He was able to ask some of the follow-up questions that promote reflection and support the practice of reasoning skills. In the end it became a good experience for everyone involved. He discovered some of the advantages of learning how to listen to others and the others found a less threatening space to express what they had in mind.

This is a good example of caring thinking within the framework of the community of philosophical enquiry, where everyone grows together and starts internalizing the skills for better thinking. Consequently everyone develops strategies for making better judgements.

The skills developed and learned in the community of philosophical enquiry are gradually internalized and then applied in other contexts outside the school setting. This can be, for example, during discussions with family or friends, or in situations that demand decision-making and require the specific circumstances of each situation to be taken into account.

In the community of philosophical enquiry, reason is recognized as practical, situated in specific contexts and requiring awareness of the consequences of our decisions; it rejects the philosophical proposals of foundationalism as well as subjectivism. Instead, the philosophical space in which students work and reflect gives a context imbued with values and centred in a participatory, caring and democratic environment.

Caring thinking extends to the way in which students act in a variety of contexts that require them to judge and take action. During adolescence there is a qualitative change in cognitive development and in the cognitive abilities of the students. The capacity for abstract thought appears in a way that had never been there before. Children are concerned about their family, their friends and school as they go into middle school and then high school; they begin to be exposed to a larger number of adults and to a variety of ways of thinking and looking at the world. They begin to realize that parents can sometimes be wrong, that they are not perfect and that other adults do not agree with many of the things that they have been told at home by their parents. Some parents allow children to see certain TV programmes, while others forbid them.

Children also interact with a larger number of teachers, not only the primary school teacher with whom they spent the whole year. They will find that some of their teachers are idealistic and want to fight actively for causes that they deem just, while other teachers will want only to get their salary regularly and be able to buy things and go on holidays once a year. Some will show interest in politics and others couldn't care less about it.

Hormonal changes and a growth in their capacity for abstract thinking come together as a window of opportunity to help students engage in discussions where they question their own values and those of their peers. They also begin to realize that they are not alone in the world and that there are other young people all over the world who do not have the same opportunities. They realize that there are places where there is child labour and exploitation and places where child soldiers are used as cannon-fodder. They also see that there is poverty and injustice in many parts of the world. They are not as sheltered and protected in the space of their homes as they were before. They begin to open their eyes to the world around them.

One of the consequences of these experiences at such a young age has to do with the development of a need to do something about things in the world that do not seem to be fair or just. In this way caring begins to extend beyond the individual person and beyond their immediate milieu. Students begin to be able to think globally. It is in the community of philosophical enquiry where we can help them to identify the strategies they need to act locally. To be not only concerned about issues of fairness and justice in the world but also to be able to do something about them at the local level can be a radically empowering thing. This could involve joining or supporting a non-governmental organization (NGO) that deals with these issues, or it could be identifying specific contexts or situations in the vicinity that could be addressed for the sake of those being treated unfairly or not having the same opportunities as others.

Adolescence is also a stage of development during which young people begin to be concerned about their future – about becoming independent and autonomous human beings. In the community of philosophical enquiry they can explore with their peers different possible avenues for constructing an individual future.

Just as caring thinking extends itself to a preoccupation for others in the world and for themselves as individuals, it also begins to create awareness about our role in our planet. Becoming critical consumers entails not only buying consciously in terms of fair trade but also a concern for the sources of production and the ways in which many of the products that we buy regularly do great harm to our environment. Discussions about sustainable development and environmental ethics should be regularly present in the topics addressed in class. This is done through the reading of short stories, videos or newspaper reports where topics on the environment are prevalent and where the groups involved suggest a variety of possible courses of action.

Collaborative thinking

Finally, the fourth dimension of higher-order thinking is collaborative thinking. Most of the features described in critical thinking, creative and caring thinking cannot happen in a vacuum and they also cannot happen individually. The sharing of opinions, the give-and-take of arguments and the exploration of alternatives, hypotheses and possible consequences of judgement can only happen collectively. That is why the collaborative aspect of the community of philosophical enquiry is essential for building reflective attitudes, tolerance and an analytical, caring mind.

Peer pressure is usually seen as a negative aspect of being an adolescent and being among adolescents. The literature talks about 'succumbing' to peer pressure. However, in the community of philosophical enquiry peer pressure can function as a positive force to ensure that commitments made for specific actions in certain areas are followed through.

So in these ways we can see that the development of higher-order thinking within the context of the community of philosophical enquiry has a very practical role, which is relevant to the lives of the young people in our care. As educators in whatever subject area we are working, the community of philosophical enquiry can advance learning because it develops meaningful contexts for the appreciation and understanding of the complexity of knowledge of whatever subject. Moreover, when we think together to explore ideas, we are in a position where we can relate those things to our lives in order to act on the findings about the topics that we have explored. This could be an attitude toward others as a consequence of an enquiry into friendship in personal, social, health and citizenship education (PSHCE), a commitment to read more as a consequence of an enquiry into the Arab–Israeli conflict in history GCSE, or to take care of the environment as a consequence of an investigation into sustainability and global warming in Year 9 geography, or to do more sports as a consequence of an enquiry into cardiovascular disease in biology A level. Whatever we, as students and teachers, commit ourselves to do as a consequence of explorations and analysis of issues that concern us, when we are able to apply our reflection and learning in the classroom to our daily lives we can become better people. This is also one of the goals of the work in the community of philosophical enquiry.

2 Identity development in adolescence: parenting styles and the community of philosophical enquiry

Identity is both a psychological construct and a philosophical construct. Psychologically it has to do with personality traits, character development and the nature of individual experiences. It is also related to the kind of parenting experienced. Philosophically, identity relates to questions like 'Who am I?' 'Why am I here?' and 'What do I want to do with my life?' The existential nature of these questions belongs more clearly within the realm of philosophy. However, there is no clear distinction between the psychological and the philosophical aspects of identity. In order to become a person one has to deal with both.

In the community of philosophical enquiry the students explore and reflect upon both aspects of identity with their peers. Gradually they envision potential answers to these questions. The questions are also related to the main objective for work in a community of philosophical enquiry, namely to develop a personal and a social project that addresses the questions of 'What kind of person do I want to be?' and 'In what kind of world do I want to live?'

Identity development in adolescence

We all have an identity from birth, but important developmental tasks start to appear at the onset of adolescence. Later on, students need to make up their minds about such things as whether to continue with formal education in school or to look for a job. They need to decide what they want to study in terms of a profession or a trade that will enable them to earn a living independently from their parents. In other words, they need to start thinking about what they will do to become autonomous and independent individuals.

It is at this stage in life that they also start building their own ideas about religion, politics, relationships and what is appropriate to do or say when they start dating.

They also begin to develop their own ideas about friendship: what constitutes a friend and what kinds of friends they want to make.

These developmental tasks are not easy for anyone who is actually experiencing adolescence. Being able to talk about their ideas and feelings at this time, and being able to explore different possible avenues of action with a group of peers, gives them a great advantage compared to others who do not share the space of a community of philosophical enquiry.

Adolescence as a discrete stage of development has been studied thoroughly only since the end of the 1960s. Erik Erikson's (1968) exploration of stages of socio-cultural development can be found in his book *Identity Youth and Crisis*, which was one of the seminal works of this time. Later on James Marcia developed an interview protocol in order to test some of Erikson's ideas about identity in adolescence.

This process of exploration and research on identity culminates with Gerald Adams and his development of the Objective Measure of Ego Identity Status, in 1979. It has been modified and improved many times since then. James Marcia has described the test as the most thoroughly developed self-report measure of the ego identity status paradigm. This self-report assessment of identity formation has now been requested for use in every continent of the world and in over 40 different countries, including democratic, socialist and communist societies, and is considered to be a great resource for research and practice. It is important to mention this because of the research that has been conducted with regard to the relationship between the development of a healthy identity during adolescence and the partici-pation in a community of philosophical enquiry during middle school and high school.

Early adolescence is understood to be the period from 10 to 13 years of age; middle adolescence is the period between 14 and 16, and late adolescence or young adulthood is from 17 to 21. Each of these stages has been identified as distinct and needing special attention regarding the specific changes that adolescents go through and the challenges they have to overcome to become autonomous human beings.

Adolescents have to make decisions about areas in their lives as they begin to 'become their own persons' – as they start developing their own goals increasingly independently of what their parents or other significant adults would like for them. Adams identifies four ideological aspects and four interpersonal aspects of identity development. The four ideological areas are choosing a vocation, ideas about politics, religion and constructing a philosophy of life. The four interpersonal ones are friendship, dating, sex-roles and recreation or use of leisure time.

Ideological dimensions of identity

Vocational choice

Vocational choice refers to the exploration that adolescents have to undertake about their strengths and weaknesses, their likes and dislikes and their goals about how to earn a living and make their own money once they leave school and become independent. As they are growing up, their ideas in terms of how to earn a living are usually unrealistic or they relate to what their parents do or what they see at home. So it is common to hear that they want to do what their parents do. When they begin to explore and discover their own interests they might decide to do something according to their real strengths and interests.

Political interests

With regard to politics, the influence of what they see and hear at home constitutes their first encounter with this important area of ideological development. They might hear that there is interest in discussing topics about sustainable development, animal rights, gender issues, criticisms of conservative or liberal political leaders in their region, or it could be that they are raised in a home setting where there is no interest in anything that has to do with political issues and ideas. Whatever the situation, the school setting and the community of philosophical enquiry will allow them to discover, discuss and reflect upon these issues, and gradually they will be able to make up their minds in terms of what they want to be committed to and how.

The emphasis on democratic values and a concern with the development of moral imagination means that issues like sustainable development and environmental ethics will definitely be present in one form or another during their discussions. The importance given to consistency between thought, word and action will hopefully ensure that they show in their actions and their behaviour that they have internalized and the ideas explored in class.

Religion

Religion is another prime example of an area that is very much influenced by what happens in the home. Children grow up adopting, at least in the beginning, the religious ideas of their home. It is when they move away from the home at somewhere between 5 and 7 years of age that the influence of school takes effect. At this point children begin to be able to compare and explore ideas that are different from their own. This offers the opportunity to make comparisons and to see that there are others who do not share the ways in which they see, for example, a religious or spiritual dimension of their lives. There will be homes where religion plays a leading part and many of the activities in the family are planned around it. There will be other homes where religion plays a minimal or no part at all. Students in a community of philosophical enquiry will eventually have to decide on their own the importance and scope that this area of ideological development is going to take.

Developing a philosophy for life

A philosophy of life is a set of beliefs that one develops and that helps guide our actions in the world. One way of finding out if adolescents are already developing a philosophy of life is by asking them to make an exercise of imagination and to describe a day in their lives in five years' and then in ten years' time. Some of the questions one can ask are:

- What do you see yourself doing in five years?
- Where do you work?
- How do you go to work? By car, bus, walking?
- How long does it take you to get there?
- Is it in a city or in a rural area?
- Is it behind a desk or in the fields?
- How are you dressed? Formally or not? Do you have to wear a uniform or not? What kinds of clothes do you like?
- Are you married? Do you have any children?
- What do you do in your free time?
- What kind of music do you listen to?
- What are your goals for the next five years?

The next step would be to ask the same questions as an exercise in imagining the situation ten years from now. This means that if adolescents are 16 they would have to imagine what their lives would be like when they are 26.

Some adolescents have a more-or-less clear idea of what they want their lives to look like in five or ten years. But there are many others for whom this exercise is very difficult or impossible to do. They have not stopped to think about their plans for the future. They do not have a clear idea of what they want to do with their lives. Many of them are unrealistic in their goal-setting because they are able to imagine a bright and successful future for themselves but they are not taking the steps necessary to make that happen. So they can say they will be successful business people and earn a lot of money but they are not having success finishing high school. A common problem is the inability of adolescents to establish the relationship between what they want to become in five or ten years and what they are doing at present. There is a kind of magical thinking where it seems that suddenly and miraculously there will be a break in their lives and they will become what they have imagined with little or no effort.

One of the functions of the community of philosophical enquiry is to inject a good dose of realism into students' thinking. While discussing issues that are important for them with their peers they are able to examine a diverse set of beliefs about things and a variety of possible actions, and also to demand from themselves the necessary consistency between word, thought and action.

The role of logic and formal reasoning plays an important part at this stage of development. Overton (1990) has described how

> by the time the child reaches his/her teens, she/he is able to reason according to rules for which formal logic might be considered to be an abstract model. But this would be true only under the condition that the reasoning is to be applied to fields in which the subjects have knowledge and experience and in situations that make sense to them ...

Developmental tasks have to do with situations and experiences that make a lot of sense to adolescents who need to think about them and tackle them in a successful manner. The nature of the changes in their cognitive development allow them to deal with cause–effect relationships, prediction of consequences and, especially important, the capacity to structure and develop short-term, medium-term and long-term goals for their life projects and to follow them through to completion.

Interpersonal dimension of identity

Within the interpersonal area of identity, adolescents have to deal with their ideas and ideals about friendship, dating, sex-roles and use of their free time, plus developing a sense of belonging to a group.

Friendship

Friendship becomes extremely important during the adolescent years. As pre-adolescents enter adolescence there is a gradual distancing from the influence of the family. Friends become increasingly important in their lives. As children become adolescents they start choosing their own friends. Young children's parents choose their friends for them, and who they are will depend upon, for example, the neighbourhood in which they live, the school they send them to and the relatives they visit and interact with. Once children begin to socialize in school and become exposed to different role-models they begin to decide whom they want to associate with or whom they want to invite home for a meal or for a weekend. Parents can influence the choice of their children's friends only to a certain point. And if they are respectful of their children's budding autonomy they might have to accept some of their friends even when they might not agree completely with their lifestyle or family and social background.

Dating

With regard to dating, young adolescents start developing closer and sometimes intimate relationships with people their own age. If their parents' relationship is healthy it is possible that they will tend to imitate those patterns of interaction, but the same is true if there is a dysfunctional family situation.

Dating starts approximately from 12 to 17, and adolescents put into practice what they think are the rules of the game and construct social roles that might accompany them for the rest of their lives. That is why the community of philosophical enquiry is so important at this stage in their lives. They will discuss with their peers what they consider appropriate or adequate and what is not. Sex education can happen best in the context of a community of philosophical enquiry, where issues like unwanted pregnancies, use of contraception, responsibility, respect for the bodies of others and for our own bodies, homosexuality and freedom can be discussed and prejudices can be challenged and questioned. Moral imagination plays an important role while discussing these issues. What would happen if ... ? What could be the consequences of ... ?

Sex-roles

Sex-roles have to do with adolescents' beliefs regarding the duties and responsibilities they have when they enter into relationships or partnerships that they intend to be more stable and long term, in many cases with the objective of forming a family and having children of their own. This stage would correspond to late adolescence – approximately 18 to 23 years of age. Here again, the influence of the parenting style is very important with regard to how they identify, clarify and negotiate these duties and responsibilities.

The way in which adolescents use their free time reflects to a great extent what their interests are and whether they have already identified a specific hobby, sport or activity that they like best. Before adolescence it is the parents who decide what to do during the free time with the family. The ability of adolescents to identify activities that they like and to spend time developing them is a part of the development of an autonomous identity. Social interaction with their peers and the variety of cultural and social activities the school setting offers will help students develop their priorities in this area.

Sense of belonging to a group

Another developmental task to be accomplished during adolescence is the acquisition of the sense of belonging to a group. Children have a strong sense of belonging to their family and their immediate community. As they enter middle and senior school they will start to identify with a variety of groups in their school or neighbourhood. A sense of belonging comes about through shared interests and values. Sometimes it includes race, belonging to an immigrant group, sharing a common religion, interest in sustainable development or an interest in peace and social justice. The community of philosophical enquiry will allow adolescents to explore the implications of belonging to one group or another. There are urban tribes that require their members to commit a crime or to harm someone belonging to an opposite group as a rite of passage. Developing moral imagination will allow students to make the most appropriate decisions for themselves and for those around them when it comes to deciding which groups are worth belonging to and which are not. There is a natural tendency for adolescents to spend more and more time with their peer groups and less with their family in this stage of development.

Adolescent identity development

There are four different categories of what Gerald Adams calls ego identity status: 'foreclosed'; 'diffuse'; 'in moratorium' and 'achieved'. Adolescents can be in any of the four categories with regard to each of the developmental tasks described above. The ideal course of identity development is when they reach an achieved identity for both the ideological and interpersonal developmental tasks.

The categories can have a dimension of crisis. When there is crisis it can manifest itself through an excessive preoccupation with things, erratic behaviour and, especially in a diffused identity, by depression and an inability to cope with everyday tasks and commitments. With regard to foreclosed identity there is no crisis because individuals in this category are sure about how they have confronted developmental tasks and are acting upon these beliefs. However, it is not an authentic identity; it is just a reflection of what others thought was best for the individual.

Children grow with the influence of the values that are shown to them at home. In most cases they obey and believe to be true what their parents tell them about right or wrong; they might or might not have a religion but there is always a set of values that families believe important to pass on to their offspring. Once they enter puberty and cognitive and hormonal changes start taking place, early, middle and late adolescents begin to question those values with which they grew up. Parents are not perfect anymore, and adolescents begin to think for themselves about issues that are important to them. Of course, the influence of value education in the family will always leave an important mark, but it does need to be questioned, reflected upon and transformed into something one owns – something that is a consequence of their own conclusions reached after careful analysis and reflection. The community of philosophical enquiry is an excellent space for accomplishing this task.

Foreclosed identity

This refers to people who have strong convictions in the areas of identity development described above but have not really reflected on the reasons why they have those convictions. Young children who do not question what they are told very much can appear to have foreclosed identities. They are responding to the influence of important and significant adults in their lives and are just doing what they were told is best for them. When they are children this is not a problem and we all have heard children who say that they want to become doctors or lawyers or teachers like their parents. When they grow to be adults, if they do not change in this respect and move into a moratorium, they will be dogmatic in their views and have a very hard time accepting criticism. When they receive criticism they typically become aggressive or they flee from situations where their views or opinions are being criticized. They are also people that seem to have an answer for every topic being discussed and an opinion about any topic under the sun. This category of identity is identified with experiences in authoritarian families.

Identity in moratorium

When values start to be questioned and analysed, adolescents enter into a moratorium. They have still not decided what to do in terms of vocation, philosophy of life, friendship, dating and all the other developmental tasks, but they are eager to explore and to search for their own answers. In the moratorium stage of identity development there is crisis, but it is a healthy crisis. It is a desire to start defining themselves as people in their own right and not only as an extension of what their parents would like them to be. There is a motivation for finding the strategies necessary to accomplish their developmental tasks. It takes time, but gradually they accomplish it and once they do they enter the stage of achieved identity. If we use vocation as an example, middle and late adolescents who are in moratorium will be finding out what their options are: either to keep on studying or to find a job. They might interview people, visit a variety of places where they would possibly want to work in the future, undertake vocational-orientation tests; and once they say 'this is it, I have really found what I want to do in terms of earning a living' they enter the achievement stage of identity development in the area of vocation.

Identity achievement

When, after careful reflection and deliberation, adolescents make a commitment with regard to their ideological and interpersonal developmental tasks, we can say they have been successful in achieving a personal identity.

However, the decisions they make at this stage are not necessarily final. They have enough flexibility of mind to be able to revise their options and to take a different course of action if they deem it necessary.

Achieved identity is not a permanent stage. There can be times and situations where they have to go back to moratorium and start investigating how to resolve a crisis that has presented itself. It could be losing their job, getting a divorce, changing religion and so forth. In worst-case scenarios they could go into a diffused identity where there can be depression and an inability to cope.

Identity diffusion

The category of diffused identity occurs when individuals are not able or willing to confront the developmental tasks of a particular stage in their lives. An example could be an adolescent who, when asked, mentions that he or she wants to keep studying but does not know what exactly. When asked if he or she is doing something to find out the response can be 'not really', or 'I don't know how', or something similar.

Diffused identity is also usually associated with a dysfunctional environment in the home – one where there is no stability and no clear guiding rules to direct adolescents in their regular behaviour and activities. This will be explored later in a discussion of parenting styles and their relation to the development of moral imagination and reasoning in the community of philosophical enquiry.

This category of diffused identity does not necessarily appear during the work adolescents do to achieve their developmental tasks. It is when there are obstacles or problems in one or more of these tasks that they can fall into a diffused identity status.

The relationship between parenting styles and development of adolescent identity

Parenting styles are closely associated with identity status and also with the ease or difficulty with which adolescents confront their developmental tasks and reach an achieved identity status. For the last 50 years there has been research and studies on the nature of the family and the influence of parenting styles in the personality development of children and adolescents. More recently, with the advent of the idea of the family as a system, large classifications have been developed to describe a variety of family systems and how they interact.

Throughout literature in the field, there have been three major classifications of parenting styles: authoritarian, indifferent inconsistent and authoritative democratic.

Authoritarian families

Authoritarian families are characterized by having clear and fixed rules regarding what is and is not allowed within the context of family life. These specify where children can go, with whom, until when, what they should and should not eat, the school they have to go to, and in extreme cases the authoritarian family also decides whom they should marry, what kind of music they should listen to, how they should dress and what they should study. They also establish clear-cut consequences for the breaking of these rules. The rules are established and decided by the parents. There is no dialogue or discussion about them and they have to be followed with no questioning. Children brought up in this kind of environment usually turn out to be obedient and docile. However, with the advent of adolescence they start to question the imposition of patterns of behaviour that allow them little space to think for themselves. It is difficult for them to become freely responsible for projects or commitments since they are always told what to do and when and how to do it. They also lack the capacity for making their own decisions because everything has always been decided for them by their parents. In terms of the identity categories described above, these children will become adolescents, and maybe adults, with a foreclosed identity. Parents do not want to see that their sons or daughters are not small children any more and they try to control their lives as if they were 10-year-olds when they could already be 25. They do not want them to enter moratorium, where they question and explore and try to find what is best for them. In terms of vocation some are told that they have to take on the family business, so they have to study something related to that business. In terms of religion they can be made to feel guilty if they deviate from what their parents' religion tells them. With regard to political standing they are seen as traitors if they differ from their parents – and so on with each of the developmental tasks that they need to achieve for themselves.

The community of philosophical enquiry, if they are lucky enough to have this space in school, will allow them to compare other parenting styles and to see that in other homes more freedom and power is given to members of the family to make their own decisions. Once adolescence begins, they might start questioning the rigidity of the rules at home. Since there is little or no dialogue in this type of family, in many cases communication is broken and relationships between parents and children become tense. In some of these homes it is possible to hear the father saying something like: 'In this household I am the one who sets the rules and as long as you live here you have to obey them; and if you don't like it you can leave.' And in some cases adolescents leave their homes in a search for more freedom and for an opportunity to form their own identity.

Some of the capacities they develop in the community of philosophical enquiry will enable them to make good decisions, even when they confront adverse circumstances. These capacities include the ability to predict the consequences of what they say and do, the ability to analyse alternative courses of action and sensibility to the contexts within which they have to make a decision.

Inconsistent, indifferent families

These families are characterized by uncertainty. Sometimes there are very strict rules and sometimes there are none. They can allow their children to go away for a weekend with their friends and then they might forbid them to go to the party one evening because it starts too late. Children growing up in this kind of environment are not enabled to hold a set of clear values about what is right or wrong. One day the father might give a child a cigarette to smoke and the next he might slap him in the face because he is smoking. Sometimes there is dialogue and sometimes there is none. Parents can show great concern for the general well-being of their children one week, while the next they ignore their needs and don't care about them. It is common for their classmates to see their situation as privileged in some ways. They can say things like: 'I wish my parents were like yours; they allow you to go anywhere at anytime and are not on top of you all the time.' And some of the young people who live in these inconsistent, indifferent households would like their parents to be more concerned and to pay more attention to them.

These families are usually dysfunctional. This means that they do not function well. There is an important distinction between a disintegrated family and a dysfunctional one. In disintegrated families it is usually the mother who heads the household and the father is absent. However, many disintegrated families function very well. And there are many integrated families, with father, mother and children sharing a household, that are very dysfunctional and that can cause children to fall into the diffuse identity category. In these families there might be problems of unemployment, alcohol or drug abuse, family violence and psychological and emotional abuse. Adolescents with diffused identities are not interested in confronting their developmental tasks and can fall into behaviours suggestive of mental illness. These adolescents have low self-esteem and are often used by their peers to engage in anti-social behaviours like stealing cars or obtaining drugs for them. They start losing interest in school and in their personal health-care, and can get up one day and watch TV for hours, eat something and keep on watching TV until they go to sleep again. These are clear signs of depression. These people are also readily influenced by whatever is in fashion in terms of sects or groups that promise them salvation, belonging and acceptance by a group of peers as long as they do what the leader says. They are prone to join urban tribes who promote and engage in anti-social behaviour.

The community of philosophical enquiry serves as a stable space for these cases. Sometimes it is the only stable place they know where they can analyse alternatives, feel accepted and respected and ask for advice from their peers. In general terms, it acts as a safe haven in the midst of the storm.

Authoritative democratic families

Finally, authoritative democratic families build a home environment that is safe and secure for their members. There is always dialogue, and children are gradually given more autonomy in making their choices and taking their own decisions. An authoritarian family will tell children what to wear every day without asking them whether they like the clothes that are chosen. In an authoritative democratic family the parent might take out three different T-shirts and ask the 4-year-old to choose the one he or she would like to wear that day. The ability to compare, contrast, reflect and make a decision is already present in this exercise. More importantly, children feel that they have a choice and that their wishes are respected and taken seriously.

As they enter adolescence, their interests become more individualistic. They might start developing their own academic interests, finding independent and creative ways of using their free time, choosing their own friends and developing their own philosophy of life. For parents in an authoritative democratic family it is a time for accompanying and advising but never demanding and forcing adolescents to do things the way they want them to. There is always dialogue and reflection and also analysis of consequences and alternatives. The possibility of conflict is always there, but they don't shy away from it. Some examples of situations that can bring about conflict have to do with some of the choices adolescents make regarding the use of tattoos, the length of their hair, sexual relations, gender orientation and leaving or not leaving school. Things are discussed in a very similar way to discussion in a community of philosophical enquiry, and in the end the adolescents carry the responsibility for the choices they make. They cannot blame others if things go wrong because it is they who make the decisions, usually with the advice and support of their parents.

This type of family encourages the passage from a foreclosed identity to a 'moratorium' and to an achieved identity in a very healthy manner for all involved. It also allows adolescents to develop an internal locus of control. This contrasts with authoritarian families, which unknowingly push their children and adolescents to grow up with an external locus of control, where they feel they have no real control over the things that happen to them and no power to design situations, plan them and accomplish what they want for their own benefit. They have been educated to obey and to do what they are told because 'grown-ups know best what is good for you and we love you'.

Adolescents in authoritative democratic families are enabled to develop their own values and to be consistent in what they think, say and do. The constant insistence on the need for consistency is found in the community of philosophical enquiry where these types of adolescents are prone to be active participants and develop strategies to defend the values that are dear to them. This space in school becomes like an extension of the way they do things in their homes, and families welcome the idea that children are given this opportunity in school.

Identity development and the community of philosophical enquiry

In summary, the development of moral imagination, especially in the period of adolescence, is best achieved if children work regularly in a community of philosophical enquiry, where they explore the kind of people they want to become and the kind of world they would like to live in. All this accompanied with the identification of the necessary strategies and steps they need to take in order to conform their personal and social projects.

In terms of identity and parenting styles, an authoritarian household will promote the development of a foreclosed identity, and this will make it difficult for an adolescent to become their own person. These families will constantly block the efforts of their adolescents to enter into a moratorium identity status and would like them to maintain the values of the family and not to construct their own.

The inconsistent, indifferent family will promote the development of a diffused identity, which is often accompanied by a lack of interest in making commitments of any kind and by a lifestyle that is concerned only with the present moment. Many of these adolescents do not have a vision of the future and are unable to postpone gratification in order to achieve medium- and long-term goals.

The authoritative democratic family sees its children and adolescents as intellectually competent and capable of engaging in reasonable dialogue. It promotes their passage from a moratorium to an achieved identity and accompanies and advises them in the various decisions that they need to make for the successful achievement of their developmental tasks.

There is no guarantee that adolescents participating in a community of philosophical enquiry will make the right choices in their lives, but they will certainly have better tools to confront the crucial decisions that face them in the twenty-first century than those who do not have the opportunity to experience this space. It will be easier for them to respond to the questions 'What kind of person do I want to be?' and 'What kind of world do I want to live in?' and to exercise the moral imagination needed to act consistently when addressing these issues.

Part 2

Hearing and Responding to the Experiences of Young People Today

3

Education and young people in the light of the impact of globalization

Global learning and education for sustainability address environmental, social and economic issues that are of importance to young people. This can make learning more relevant to their lives and have a positive impact on engagement and achievement. Working towards sustainable development goals can also increase the sense of purpose felt by young people as they develop into responsible citizens. (Qualifications and Curriculum Authority)

The experience of adolescence in the face of globalization

Globalization has given young people many opportunities to encounter others and their lifestyles from all over the world, both in real life and in the virtual worlds of the internet and television. Perhaps for the first time in history new technologies have also opened up opportunities for us to envision a more just and equitable world.

This ease of communication has allowed young people to dream of many different ways in which they could choose to live their lives. From the cities of New York, Accra and Mexico, London, Mumbai and Beijing to rural areas of Cumbria in the north of England, rural farms of Texas, remote villages in Burma and Italy, to the highlands of Chiapas on the border of Mexico and Guatemala, where indigenous communities live close to the earth – all are watching globalized TV programmes. Television markets the globalized lifestyle of Nike trainers, drinks from Coca-Cola and Nestlé, cars from Ford and Volkswagen, clothes from Wal-Mart and Tesco. These possible ways of life are very alluring; however, young people are also increasingly aware of the paradoxical nature of this globalization.

There is another problem for the young people who live comfortably in Europe. From inside Europe there is a false vision of just how difficult things are 'out there'.

There is a kind of veil between most of Europe and the rest of the world. It could perhaps be called an economic curtain. It is invisible from the European side but almost impenetrable from the other. The growth in the debt of the developing world has been well documented and this has had a huge impact on opportunities for the young people there. Decades ago psychologists realized that to lead a healthy, successful life it was necessary to be able to predict the future based on past events. Some degree of security about the future is essential to good mental health (Kelly 1955). It would seem that the need to make sense, to find meaning in our experience, is essential for human beings. It is therefore important that we create educational experiences that facilitate teachers and students in piecing together these kinds of meaning in their lives.

Economic globalization

Although it is true that in the fast-growing economies of China and India there have been benefits for some in terms of improved job and educational opportunities, people in the wealthy industrial nations have 'benefited' proportionally much more through greater ease of access to a wider variety of much cheaper products. Alongside this, an increasing economic gap has developed between the rich and the poor. Many young people are being left behind, completely outside the economic boom experienced in the industrialized nations. Young people from farming families or the children of artisans making traditional clothes, potters and weavers, those with traditional skills that served their communities well for generations, are being lost. How do we expect adolescents from these families – who have access to the TV, who see the material prosperity available to some but completely out of their reach, to respond?

The world has entered a paradoxical helix with an upward spiral of over-consumption and unimaginable wealth for some and a parallel downward spiral of poverty and hunger for the majority of others. What kind of a world do we want to prepare our young people for? Will it be one of continued unsustainable over-consumption, of biological and environmental destruction, or a different kind of world where young people have the skills to resolve conflict and build a just system for all? How are we preparing our young people to deal with the changes that will come when economic and material uncertainties start to face us all in more equal measure?

When young people have the means to reflect clearly on the values they see and the ones they want to take forward we will be more certain of a secure future for all.

When machines and computers, profit motives and property rights are considered more important than people; the giant triplets of racism, militarism, and economic exploitation are incapable of being conquered. A true revolution of values will soon cause us to question the fairness and justice of many of our present policies ... (Martin Luther King, Jr)

How would you and your students respond to the challenge of a 'true revolution of values' put to us by Martin Luther King?

Cultural globalization

Another kind of globalization has also been taking place, which has had a direct and immediate impact on the adolescents of today. This is a globalization of culture, which is influencing young people's tastes in clothes, music and food in many parts of the world. It is a by-product of economic globalization and increased consumerism and consumption. Adolescents around the world aspire to the image created by globalized companies with respect to their mobile phones, their dress options, their music preferences and so on. These companies create images. Young people often think they have free choices about their identities; however, the truth may be rather different as they are manipulated by advertising and the deliberate creation of alternative but commercially constructed images. Without the development of capacities for critical thought, young people will be directed into adulthood by companies keeping track of their purchasing decisions in ways beyond the imagination of previous generations. This globalization of culture often stands in tension with other culturally specific boundaries, as can be illustrated by questions raised by adolescent girls choosing to wear the *hijab* and or *niquab*. 'The right thing to do' is no longer clear.

Issues of the globalization of culture have been further complicated by the rise in international travel. Three generations ago only the rich or very well-educated had the opportunity or inclination to travel. Other changes have brought an increasing movement of people across the world, especially in Europe. As a consequence of this increased travel and migration, young people today are likely to meet much more frequently with people from a wide variety of backgrounds. It is essential to prepare young people for life in a pluralistic world containing many cultures.

Having knowledge of other cultural backgrounds and beliefs will not be sufficient to navigate through an increasingly culturally complex world. It will be essential for education to offer opportunities for young people to develop the skills and attitudes of understanding and open-mindedness for this new world. In the face of difference and uncertainty, young people will need to be able to have opportunities to form their own identities at a time when communities are more fractured and disparate.

We know that one of the key tasks of adolescence is to construct a complete, integrated identity that enables them to function as responsible, healthy mature adults. To do this there is the need to develop strong interpersonal skills that will enable them to handle the complexity of relationships in which they will find themselves engaged.

We would seek to argue here that a key responsibility of education, and for us as educationalists, is to support young people on this journey. It cannot be enough simply to direct young people to success in examinations. There are greater requirements and responsibilities of national and global education systems.

International responses to the impact of globalization on adolescents

The World Bank reported on the situation of young people in the world today in its World Development Report of 2007 and is expressing concern for the youth of the world. There is awareness that the situation of the globally disenfranchised youth of the poorest cities of the world raises many ethical questions for the whole world in terms not only of economic justice but also international security. These young people, disempowered and disenfranchised today, could become the terrorists of the future. In contrast to the disenfranchisement that is taking place around the world, research evidence shows that countries that invest in better education, health-care and job training for the now record numbers of young people between the ages of 12 and 24 will produce better economic growth and will have a strategic influence on reducing poverty. The World Bank report therefore seeks to encourage developing countries to spend more funds upon education in order to prepare the next generation for full participation in the global society.

Critics of the World Bank's concern suggest, however, that the care that it has expressed for the adolescents of the world is not a genuine concern for justice and faith in a common humanity but that it comes from a concern to further the new 'neoliberal' agenda. In this context we understand 'neoliberalism' as that 'set of theoretical principles and ... socio-political practices ... which are directed toward extending and deepening capitalist market relations in most spheres of our social lives' (Sukarieh and Tannock 2008).

Looking at the way the world has changed in recent decades, a strong argument could be made for saying that the well-being that seemed to have been developing around the world in the years after the Second World War, between 1950 and 1970, has been reversed and that there has been a re-establishment of power and economic advantage for a few. Some would go as far as to suggest that there has been some intentional re-establishing of power and reversal of some of the intention of the reordering of the global economies which took place after the Second World War with the aim of stabilizing the world after the crisis of the 1930s and 1940s. As educationalists we should not avoid reflecting upon these things and the part we have to play in education of the next generation of global citizens.

Education for the twenty-first century in the shadow of globalization

An alternative to the kind of response represented by the World Bank is to develop an education structure that could bring forward a new generation of adults who participate fully in the systems in which they find themselves. These people will have the skills of critical thought to appreciate and understand what is happening in the world and they will have the social and interpersonal skills to resolve problems without conflict.

Preparing young people for life in this new world is not going to be an easy task. It will require much more than simply teaching and learning facts about another religion or another culture. It has to be much more than simply touring other countries, eating exotic food or celebrating foreign festivals. It will not be enough simply to learn a few phrases of a foreign language, or to watch foreign films, or to chat online with foreign students. Adolescents growing into responsible global citizens in the global village need to develop high-level capabilities in order to be able to reflect critically about what they see. If there is to be an authentic empathy and respect there will have to be a kind of awakening of conscience, a moral conscience that refuses to accept the injustices that the negative aspects of globalization are bringing into our world.

A global citizen understands difference, can manage complexities, and can productively live and work across cultures. This kind of 'global citizenship' can only develop through sustained deep engagement with other cultures. It may involve them engaging in direct and perhaps sometimes confrontational interactions with other peoples. It is often, of course, through careful and sometimes frustrating examination of ourselves in the face of people with a different 'cosmo-vision' or 'worldview', who believe in a different god or no god, who have different ways of living and who speak different tongues that we discover who we are and become confident in our difference.

Richard Rorty, a modern philosopher writing in the pragmatist tradition, addressed the UNESCO philosophy forum in 1996. He suggested that to find answers to the greatest problems of our time we must look again at the nature of humankind. We must ask ourselves the question 'Who are we?' Are we individuals working alone for our own interest? Or in reality are we social beings who are totally dependent upon each other for our well-being. In as much as one person thrives we all thrive, in as much as one community suffers we all suffer. This is not poetry or religion but a moral question that we need to consider. Showing young people how to recognize compelling moral questions and giving them experience of working with compelling moral arguments is surely essential in a contemporary education system.

Rorty himself suggests that this question will be important for our time as it begins to address the political dimension. The political is used here in the Greek sense of *polis*: as something which we are all responsible for engaging in. Those working with the community of philosophical enquiry are comfortable with including the political into our enterprise. The community of philosophical enquiry, through advancing environments of reasonable dialogue, seeks to nurture the values essential for the well-being of a sustainable democracy. These will include respect, acceptance of difference and the willingness to compromise to build a shared response to a problem. Young people who have had experience of the community of philosophical enquiry over time develop greater capacity to handle ambiguity and to be able to listen to each other without needing to dominate others with their point of view. Young people who have had the opportunity to work in this way over time are more open to new possibilities, more able to think imaginatively and to take creative risks in their thinking and to make good judgements based on careful reasoning – skills we consider to be essential to the survival of our kind on this planet and essential to build a good and just world for all.

Peter Singer in his book *The Life You Can Save* (2009) suggests that something has happened to more or less disengage our moral thinking and reflecting. He argues that many of us in industrialized countries have things we do not need and that there is a moral argument for us to give much more to the poor. If this were done then we could resolve poverty, and his book suggests that if we were to think and reflect more deeply upon the moral arguments as to why we should give to the poor we would feel compelled to do it and would in fact be much more likely to act. In other words, if everyone were to reflect philosophically and with rigour we would change people's actions and resolve poverty; as for Singer there is a transparent link between the capacity to reason well and the capacity to act. There are of course arguments for and against the possibility of charity versus amending international policy as the way to resolve poverty. Singer is certainly challenging people to think and research deeply.

> To live is to choose. But to choose well, you must know who you are and what you stand for, where you want to go and why you want to get there. (Kofi Annan)

How far can we support young people to engage with this kind of deep learning? And can we afford not to?

Globalization and the well-being of teenagers

If we do not listen and respond to the voice of the young people in our care the well-being of the next generation could be in question. According to the UNICEF study *Child Poverty in Perspective* (2007) young people in Britain are among the most unhappy in the world. There have been grave concerns about the anxiety levels of pre-school children in the UK, and we know that young British people take more risks in terms of alcohol, drugs and sexual behaviour than young people in other parts of Europe. The *Good Childhood* report from the Children's Society (2009) suggests that the greatest danger to children and young people in Britain today is the individualism of adults. It suggests that most of the obstacles that children face today are linked to the belief among adults that people's prime duty is to make the most of their own lives, rather than contributing to the good of others. In the community of philosophical enquiry young people learn to work with others to build on the ideas of their peers and, in so doing, learn that often the most useful ideas are those that have been co-constructed and whose development has been shared together with a shared consideration of the outcomes.

How the community of philosophical enquiry can contribute to emotional well-being and support healthy perceptions of the other

There has been considerable work on the contribution that the community of philosophical enquiry can make to the well-being of primary-age children. For example, in the primary social and emotional aspects of learning (SEAL) materials there is a large amount of discussion about this, with help for teachers as they plan their work on their students' emotional development. The work at Gallions School in London in recent years serves as an example of good practice in this field. This school opened in 1999 in an area of London that has a high level of deprivation and need. The community of philosophical enquiry, in the form of Philosophy for Children (P4C), was introduced as part of the school's work with Antidote, an organization that seeks to advance emotional literacy in the curriculum. The aim was to offer children time to think and talk about things that really matter to them. Here the children were given an opportunity to reflect on how the philosophy programme in school has helped them. David says that he thinks philosophy has changed him a lot. He says how

> In Year 3 I was always angry, I used to cry really a lot, I'm not saying I don't do it now in Year 6, but not as much as I used to. In Year 3, I always wanted to get my own way. Now I've learned how to listen to different people's opinions and it's changed me, I'm not so angry no more.

Another student has expressed a real liking for philosophy because it's a time to say what you believe and to listen to other people's opinions. Philosophy is different from other subjects because the key is listening to everybody's opinions.

It is important to reflect upon emotional development when considering introducing philosophical enquiry into schools; however, it is important that the work does not stop there. Philosophy for children was not intended as a therapeutic programme; emotional well-being is important, but in this context only as part of something bigger and more significant. In reality it offers something more complex and entirely educationally relevant. Working in the community of philosophical enquiry there is the opportunity to weave together both emotional and cognitive ways of thinking. Young people can become more able to make sound judgements based on good reasoning. The work in the community of philosophical enquiry does not preclude examining feelings in the way that a regular scientific enquiry might, but it cannot be the end-point or main aim. When working with one's peers on a topic of great relevance, it can be beneficial to learn to think clearly about something that in another context could generate strong emotions. This is where the potential for empowerment to change behaviour comes from.

Research evidence is showing that thinking philosophically with one's peers can change not only perception of violence but action in response to those perceptions. Daniel, Doudin and Pons (2006) found that very young children's perception of violence or of pre-violent situations can be sensitized though regular working in the community of philosophical enquiry. It has been suggested that the possibility of working with difference through language by thinking philosophically can facilitate the growth in cognitive competencies which in turn facilitate the development of understanding and tolerance of different points of view. This can lead to a growing ability to appreciate that there can be more than one viewpoint on many matters. In fact a failure to appreciate this can lead to inner confusion and irritation in the face of perceived difference, which can itself lead to aggression.

We must ask how this could apply in the secondary school. It has been reported elsewhere (Williams and Wergerif 2006) that students who have had the opportunity to participate in regularly philosophical enquiry and have had the opportunity to reflect philosophically on values that this impacts not just on the self regulation of the students within the enquiry but that it can spill out into the general ethos of the whole school. As experience with philosophical enquiry grows, as the relationship with the teacher develops into one of guide and shared thinker, so respect for the other spreads out from the classroom into other situations.

Where there is the possibility of building on the work of our colleagues in the primary school, this will bring great advantage. Clearly if young people are coming into the secondary school ready to listen to each other, to put their own egos in perspective and to appreciate that there could be another point of view on a matter, then we will be a long way along the road to making thoughtful reflective secondary classrooms.

We will need to work with young people, emphasizing the importance of clear and reasonable thinking. We can support them to become more open to the possibility that they may be mistaken and that not every opinion is equally likely to be correct. But how can we do this? The facilitator in the secondary classroom will need to be a very skilful person indeed. When the work of the facilitator is taken seriously and the teacher practises how she listens to the development of the enquiry, she will become increasingly able to listen carefully for problems such as inconsistencies or poor logic. She will ask a student to self reflect when she challenges them by saying, 'Does that really follow from what you said earlier?' She can suggest to the whole class that they think carefully when she asks whether the group 'agrees with John when he says that x must be the case.' The teacher/facilitator will have noticed that there was an inconsistency in the contributions to the enquiry and will feed back to the group how he noticed that an earlier part of the conversation was suggesting the opposite. It is the responsibility of the facilitator to guide the conversation to ensure that the philosophical concepts are well explored and clarified. Distinctions will be made between different terms so that the work of the investigation into the question chosen by the young people in the group, develops greater clarity and those participating in the enquiry develop higher thinking capabilities.

Our hypothesis here is that as young people work over time with the community of philosophical enquiry they will come to understand better who they are in the world in relation to others and can begin to handle the stresses of living in a globalized world not by defending against it or closing down in the face of its immensity but rather by facing and taking responsibility for its well-being. Being able to think clearly can help greatly with all manner of problems. In the community of philosophical enquiry, strategies for problem solving can be rehearsed. This is not a quick-fix methodology. It will need to be built into the curriculum and designed into the whole-school policy over the whole length of time a student is in a school.

> Societies aren't made of sticks and stones, but of people whose individual characters, by turning the scale one way or another; determine the direction of the whole. (Plato, *The Republic*).
>
> How can we engage students in the governance of every level of school activity so that they can be responsible citizens of today? Do schools need to change?

Personalized learning and student voice

In recent years there has been a growing awareness that in a knowledge economy there needs to be a new focus on learning rather than on the input of knowledge alone. Moving to a new culture where young people are supported in learning how to learn, where they are supported in developing the skills needed for the future, and where these things become the central work of schools, will take time. However those of us working in schools right now know that the change has to come faster than is probably comfortable. There are many questions and there is much uncertainty ahead.

The development of a 'student voice' in a school has to be much more than just bolting on a school council to the work of an already busy institution. An awareness of the deep needs of adolescents must to be woven into the fabric of the school. Philosophical thinking can be embedded into every aspect of the life of a school, with the skills of investigation and enquiry being developed in the more formal area of classroom practice. To really personalize the learning opportunities in a school there needs to be a changing culture where the life of each human being is valued and regarded.

This will be developed further below where we explore how young people can be empowered to act to change the things in the world that may not be healthy rather than just coping with them when they begin to think critically and in collaboration with others, they can be empowered to act to change the things in the world that may not be healthy rather than just coping with them.

If nature has made any one thing less susceptible than all others of exclusive property, it is the action of the thinking power called an idea, which an individual may exclusively possess as long as he keeps it to himself but the moment it is divulged, it forces itself into the possession of everyone, and the receiver cannot dispossess himself of it. Its peculiar character, too, is that no one possesses the less, because every other possesses the whole of it.

He who receives an idea from me, receives instruction himself without lessening mine; as he who lights his taper at mine, receives light without darkening me. That ideas should freely spread from one to another over the globe, for the moral and mutual instruction of man, and improvement of his condition, seems to have been peculiarly and benevolently designed by nature, when she made them, like fire, expansible over space, without lessening their density at any point, and like air in which we breathe, move, and have our physical being, incapable of confinement or exclusive appropriation. Inventions then cannot, in nature, be a subject of property. (Thomas Jefferson)

How can we transform our schools into communities of philosophical enquiry where the community of the school becomes a shared living experience?

4 Building on hope, reforming the curriculum

To have risked so much in our efforts to mould nature to our satisfaction and yet to have failed in achieving our goal would indeed be the final irony.

So wrote Rachel Carson in her seminal book, *Silent Spring*, published in 1962. This book exposed the destruction of wildlife as a result of the widespread use of DDT and other pesticides. She drew attention to the fragility and interconnectedness of the environment upon which we all depend. Her insights led to the banning of DDT and the careful monitoring of the use of chemicals, which we now assume to be happening around the world. It marked the beginning of the environmental movement as we know it and the book itself is considered by many as having changed the course of history.

Recent responses to climate change

Many years after Carson's book was published we do not seem to have learned as much as we might have hoped. The independent Stern review (Stern 2006) was commissioned by the Chancellor of the Exchequer in the UK to report to both the Chancellor and to the Prime Minister in order to assess the evidence and build an understanding of the economics of climate change. Its major conclusion was that there is an overwhelming body of scientific evidence that clearly indicates *climate change is a serious and urgent issue*. The Earth's climate is changing rapidly, mainly as a result of increases in greenhouse gases caused by human action. The report goes on to suggest that most climate models show that *a doubling of preindustrial levels of greenhouse gases is very likely to commit the Earth to a rise of between 2°C and 5°C in global mean temperatures*. This level of greenhouse gases will probably be reached between 2030 and 2060. A warming of 5°C on a global scale would be far outside the experience of human civilization and comparable to the difference between temperatures during the last Ice Age and today. Several new studies suggest up to a 20 per cent chance that warming could be greater than 5°C.

A sustainable society has been described as one that can take care of itself without putting future generations at risk. This has to be a society that is at peace with itself and one that has reached a just way of living. The consequences of climate change seem most likely to be neither just nor peaceful. Civil war and other violent situations are increasing globally and the links between the wars, for example, in Ethiopia and the Sudan have been well documented as being related to climate change and the consequent need for government intervention to advance sustainable economic development (Sachs 2007, 2009). A responsible education system will need to take into account the practical implications of climate change and also find ways of working with adolescents and engaging their developing moral perception of the world.

The possible catastrophic impact of climate change has been in the public domain for a very long time. Nations convened at the Rio de Janeiro Earth summit in 1992 agreed that contemporary social trends were not sustainable. Yet soil depletion, overfishing and pollution of many kinds continued through the 1990s and the early part of the twenty-first century. This relentless destruction continued at such a pace that, for example, at the 2002 summit in Johannesburg it was confirmed that in the ten years since the Rio summit few practical changes had been made to global lifestyles.

The Stern review was a genuine attempt to bring about the rapid response needed to unite the collective energy of world governments, non-governmental organizations and the globalized companies – the interests of whom can be represented by institutions such as the World Trade Organization, the World Bank and the International Monetary Fund. Educationists, too, must surely have a responsibility to work together across the globe to ensure that our education systems are preparing young people for the reality of the future that they will face.

Violent consequences of climate change

Most scientists agree that there is a direct connection between the many violent situations in the world today and the already apparent effects of climate change. For example, the failure of normal and anticipated rainfall in sub-Saharan Africa has contributed not only to famines and chronic hunger but also to the onset of violence, when hungry people clash over scarce food and water. When violence erupts in water-starved regions such as Darfur, Sudan, political leaders tend to view the problems in narrow political terms. If they act at all, they mobilize peacekeepers, international sanctions and humanitarian aid. Where conflict and social unrest is found there will undoubtedly be underlying causes of great poverty and social injustice.

It could be argued that several other areas of conflict that have developed during the early years of the twenty-first century have occurred as a result of attempts to secure energy supplies for the already developed powerful Western nations, to allow more consumption. Given what is already known about the dangers of continued burning of fossil fuels, these events are incredible. We should be indignant that our governments condone actions that encourage conflicts between human beings so that they can secure power over resources, rather than working together to formulate and implement possible solutions to our current global problems. If international agencies fail to work to mitigate future climate change, the effects of rising temperatures, increasing droughts, more numerous and severe tropical storms, rising sea-levels and a spread of tropical diseases will pose a huge threat to the entire planet. The famines in Ethiopia and the violence in Darfur give just a flavour of what can lie ahead (Sachs 2009).

The issues of peace, justice and sustainable living on our planet can be seen to be inextricably linked. The topics developed in the classroom will need to be formally connected as well as for new links to emerge in the enquiring classroom. In this way deep and meaningful learning that may impact on the way in which people live their lives can be enabled to take place.

In so many ways we seem to be like civilizations that have gone before us – the Mayans, the Romans and the Easter Islanders. These peoples were also unable to change their behaviour, unable to take into account the consequences of their actions, before the sudden fall of their known ways of life. It seems that the Mayans, for example, may have continued to burn acres of forest to provide fuel for the stucco needed for their important buildings long after it was clear they were bringing unsustainable pressure on the planet. Jared Diamond has discussed these matters well in his recent book, *Collapse*. However, he does offer us some hope in his examination of civilizations that *were* able think ahead about the consequences of their actions and to change ways of behaving. For example, there were those who were able to challenge assumptions about the way things were done and about the way the world was, and who were able to take risks for the common good rather than for individual interests. The challenges before us are immense – but another world is possible.

Climate change: a consequence of overconsumption and globalization

The problems that globalization and overconsumption are bringing to us, in the main, come as a result of the inability of human beings to think through the consequences of their own actions and to modify behaviour. Many examples can be cited here, including deforestation and large-scale flooding of valleys for hydroelectric schemes across the world, which in fact cause increased carbon dioxide and therefore relate to climate change. What are our young people to make of the inconsistent and illogical example of their elders?

We must look for explanations for this situation to our almost fatal detachment from and lack of awareness of our complete dependence upon the natural world. This, together with the loss of traditional knowledge regarding our interdependence and interrelationship with the Earth and the progressive industrialization of the occidental lifestyle. We may rightly puzzle at the extent to which we have become separated from the production of our basic necessities and how we have arrived at such excessive consumerism.

This lack of thought about our overconsumption has led us to a precipice. The question now is whether we can reconnect all the pieces necessary for the sustaining of human life on the planet in all its complexity in order to move towards a just existence for everyone. Whether we will able to modify our behaviour in time seems to be a matter for discussion. However, for all of us involved in education it seems imperative to try.

Education for sustainable development

The UNESCO Decade for Education for Sustainable Development was launched in 2005 and is achieving some significant international recognition. It is building on many years of work in the field of environmental education and recognizes the urgency for effective education that can alter our current behaviours. In recent decades many different models of environmental education have been developed. In light of the relentless human impact on the Earth, we should reflect further upon the reasons for the lack of effectiveness of these programmes. There is a realization that there must be coordination of educational efforts in this area (see for example the 'Asia–Pacific Guidelines for the Development of National ESD Indicators', UNESCO 2006); however, we suggest that a new approach is needed in order to move people who are comfortable in their existing lifestyles to question radically many assumptions about life. Change involving realization of personal responsibility is hard under any circumstances, but when this is combined with an awareness that we need to change in concert with others, the situation seems even harder to resolve.

There is, of course, also a grave need for informed international political action to halt our destruction. All too often international meetings are proving less than successful with the desires of some for shared understanding and changed behaviours being frustrated by the actions of governments that are acting solely in their own interest, unable to move to a more sustainable position (see, for example, the Climate Change negotiation in 2001 and World Trade Negotiations of 2008). However, if we seek to identify a responsible ethical framework for society, and if we hope to communicate the world vision implicit in this ethical framework to the next generation, we must ensure there is congruence in our educational structures between *what* we hope to build and *how* we plan to do this. There needs to be a process that brings together the knowledge that people have about what is happening to our planet and the emotional and psychological factors that must also be in place to put people in a position where they are able to determine their own actions and change the way they live.

This is all so much harder when we are living in such a time of uncertainty. Teachers themselves are human beings and face the same dilemmas in their lives as the students in the classrooms. In the UK we have been given a National Curriculum and with the accompanying pressures of standardized assessment tests, league tables of schools and Ofsted, there has been little incentive to move towards change. However, there are signs that this is changing. Ofsted in England is now requiring schools to report on their moves towards a global dimension and also to demonstrate on their self-evaluation forms how they are implementing the Sustainable School framework. In this way schools are being called to account for the way in which they are progressing in implementing moves towards sustainability.

What are the skills needed to develop a sustainable lifestyle?

Nobel Prize-winning author Alexander Solzhenitsyn, who chronicled Soviet repression and exposed Stalin's labour camp system to the world, died in 2008 at the age of 89. In June 1975, during a prophetic Harvard address, he said:

> The split in today's world is perceptible even to a hasty glance. [We can readily] identify two world powers, each of them already capable of entirely destroying the

other. However, understanding the split often is limited to … the illusion that danger may be abolished through successful diplomatic negotiations or by achieving a balance of armed forces. The truth is that the split is a much profounder and a more alienating one, that the rifts are more than one can see at first glance. This deep manifold split bears the danger of manifold disaster for all of us, in accordance with the ancient truth that a Kingdom – in this case, our Earth – divided against itself cannot stand. (Solzhenitsyn 1975)

The untenable divisions observed in the world by Solzhenitsyn have become increasingly complex since his address. The skills that young people will need during their adult lives will be those that enable them to handle this increasing complexity.

The advent of the information age has meant that information is available from many sources. In order to be fully empowered in one's life and to be prepared to live in a democratic society, a responsible adult will be need to be able to handle these different information sources, or at least know how to. More than a million books are published globally each year, and the internet streams a vast amount of information into people's homes. For those young people who will take on positions of leadership, a high level of literacy and other research and information-handling skills will be needed in order for them to read and digest different types of information. They will also need the ability to extract information and distinguish relevant from irrelevant information for particular purposes. In other words, the skills of critical and discerning thinking will be essential.

In addition to this vast amount of information, there are many different systems at work in the world. For example, health-care systems, legal systems, insurance and government taxation systems. In order for young people to be able to take care of themselves and their families, an ability to master these different systems will be desirable. The systems are codified, so an ability to decipher codes and understand and appreciate different languages in different systems will be needed.

In many European societies there has been large-scale migration recently – for many reasons, including economic migration due to the expansion of the European Union. However, there is also migration of refugees due to violence in other parts of the world and this migration can create more difficulties in a society and challenge the local population. Young people becoming the adults of tomorrow will need to be able to understand, appreciate and accept different cultures and ways of life. They will need to be able to think reasonably and in an informed way about the realities of migration in order to build societies that are whole and not fragmented. An ability to live with difference and ambiguity in terms of culture will be essential and the qualities of character necessary for this can be cultivated through the work of the community of philosophical enquiry.

It has been argued that the skills needed for young people of the future will be primarily cognitive in order to handle the increasing information. These skills will clearly be important but in addition far greater emphasis should be placed upon the development of social and inter-human skills in order to be able to handle the new complexities of social life due to the great changes in the working of the world. As discussed above, the globalization of culture has given young people new options about social behaviour. However, we must also support young people in their development as secure social beings who are able to form secure relationships as they bring forward the next generation. The effects of family breakdown can be observed on the streets of many cities – with increased gun and knife crime in the UK for example. In the cities of Latin America there has for a long time been social and family breakdown with many negative consequences of drug and alcohol use.

Margaret Mead (2001), writing in the 1920s, talked about the need for education for choice. Clearly this remains an important element of education, but there needs to be a new moral element here. Choice cannot be exactly free and individualistic. We need, as Rorty encourages us, to look not only for the best option for ourselves as individuals but for the best option for ourselves as participants in a large life project. This, in turn, requires us to take into consideration the nature of the reality of the whole planet.

So to develop our young people on their way to becoming adults of the future will need skills of negotiation, of collaboration. Working out how we are going to live in a global community will not be something that can be undertaken alone.

Learning *about* sustainability will not be sufficient; we need to find ways to heal the economic and cultural divisions. We will need to bring together the rational and the emotional, the material and the spiritual. The task ahead for education in the global community is to do this in a democratic way that can tolerate ambiguity and celebrate difference. We need to find processes that will allow our young people to develop a new vision of morality – one that nurtures imagination but can also connect imagination and action, so that their visions of life and their lifestyles are working in congruence.

In a classroom that is modelled on and informed by the work of the community of philosophical enquiry, over time, an atmosphere develops that is conducive to democratic thinking and working. It will be a classroom where difference and diversity will be supported and explored. The aim of this philosophical exploration is not to find out which one end-view is the 'best' and so to place that in an author-itarian position above all others. Rather the work of the philosophical and enquiring classroom allows for a sensitive exploration of many points of view, for things to be examined and challenged and for a shared resolution to be achieved for 'the time being'. Over time, students who become familiar with working in the community of philosophical enquiry develop an increased capacity to tolerate ambiguity and uncertainty. They become better at hypothetical reasoning and at the same time develop their capacity to think in a variety of reasonable ways and to consider philosophical implications of holding one point of view over another. Not all opinions can be considered as equally valid. This is not relativism but neither is it the authoritarian absolutism so often presented in more didactic, formal classrooms. We live in a time of uncertainty; we are looking, therefore, for probability, for an ability to tolerate a certain degree of ambiguity and to hold more than one possibility in mind at any one time. This is intelligent thinking which allows flexibility to change depending on the information available. These will be essential skills for survival and they are at the heart of creativity.

How can the curriculum be amended to give scope for these skills to develop?

All learners need to acquire the necessary skills, knowledge base, values and attitudes from the outset to be active global citizens in creating a sustainable society. This is predominately addressed through developments in curricula, pedagogy and experience. (http://www.learning.wales.gov.uk/pdfs/esdstrategye.pdf.)

New curricula being developed in the occidental world are beginning to show an awareness of the need to respond to the future facing us. In the UK new curricula have been published and implemented recently, claiming to want to develop responsible citizens who are capable of building just societies.

The Leitch report (Leitch 2006) was designed to consider the skills that are necessary to ensure economic well-being and continued development of social justice in a democracy such as that of the UK. It considers that efforts should be made to dismantle the barriers that prevent people from completing the level 2 standard of education in order to ensure the well-being of the whole community (level 2 is the standard of five GCSE passes or equivalent, normally achieved at 16 years of age in the UK). The main barrier is considered to be low aspiration of the kind that can be passed from generation to generation unless deliberate action is taken. The Leitch report also recognizes that those without this level of education are the most likely to be caught in poverty. Clearly in all educational institutions we need to be working hard to raise aspiration. Where there is hope and belief in the value of education there will be attainment.

There are many fine words about *what* is needed for the future – about what kinds of citizens we need to develop – but is given little guidance or thought as to *how* these things are to be achieved. The most important work that the teacher in the community of philosophical enquiry has to do is to create a democratic space where important issues in the form of philosophical questions can be developed and investigated through the tools that philosophy has to offer. The teacher becomes a facilitator of the conversation or the dialogue between the members of the community gathered in the classroom. It is imperative that the teacher becomes a person who can be pedagogically strong and yet remain philosophically humble. This means teachers become skilled and crafted educators who can listen carefully to the voices of the young people in the classroom over a period of time. They will not be the kind of teacher who seeks to present their own opinion as if it were the only view. Instead, this kind of teacher will be open to listening to many different points of view, but will have the pedagogical strength to bring out the best philosophical arguments. Through this work the teacher will facilitate the development of the skills necessary for a deep understanding of the nature of current problems through serious dialogue.

The way the teacher/facilitator supports the development of the questions will enable students to develop stronger reasoning capabilities. This will bring greater confidence and assurance and at the same time develop habits of mind that are more patient and calm. Facilitators will encourage young people to give examples and to identify contradictions. They will support the community as they search for alternatives and soon the students themselves will begin to be able to predict the consequences of following one line of investigation rather than another. In so doing students themselves will develop greater capacity to suggest possible inferences and to spot moments when incorrect inferences are being made. They will gradually develop a greater congruence in their thinking. New pieces of information will be able to be considered in the light of previous experience. This is intelligent thinking, flexible thinking, creative thinking. These will be the skills essential for navigating peacefully in times when the future is uncertain.

Ultimately, young people will be empowered to consider the kind of people that they would like to become. They will be less influenced by advertising and by their peers. They will be able to make reasoned decisions that take account of emotional considerations but are not swayed by them alone. The community of philosophical enquiry, as we have seen, facilitates the development of a strong sense of personal identity – something that is essential at this time in the development of the adolescent. However, even more powerfully, this work with philosophy in the community of their peers facilitates young people to envision the kind of world in which they would like to live. This is the work of the creative imagination.

Considering the role of creativity and of imagination in developing a more just and fair world, and one which offers the possibility of sustainable life for us all, is the task of the next chapter.

5   Education for a global imagination

This chapter brings together all the preceding chapters. It links recent national and international moves to reform the school curriculum with other (e.g. from Europe and UNESCO) initiatives, and it then makes a case for a key role for philosophy in secondary schools.

Curriculum reform in the face of globalization

Major challenges face education policy-makers throughout the world as they envision education fit for the twenty-first century. Such education must support intelligent changes in behaviour in the light of globalization, overconsumption, environmental degradation and climate change.

Curriculum documents published in many counties in the past few years claim to address the learning requirements of students in the twenty-first century. They move away from rote-learning towards more a more skills-based, concept-based and competence-based curriculum. Despite important changes there remains a focus on teacher guidance of the knowledge framework for examination success.

However, we live in an information age – a knowledge society – and most young people living a globalized lifestyle have access to huge amounts of information each moment of every day. They are connected to many different sources of knowledge and information: computer messaging systems, blogs, networking sites such as 'Facebook', discussion groups, iPods, mobile phones and so on. They need skills to help them make good judgements regarding what knowledge is worth having and acting upon and what could well be ignored. Adults may not figure much in this youthful knowledge-gathering and therefore can offer little guidance on these things; however, through dialogue with their peers on messaging sites young people have the possibility to develop and fine-tune their sense of place in the world within a particular context.

How many different kinds of electronic equipment do the young people you teach each day work with? How many of these enable them to communicate with the knowledge society? What good reasons could there be for removing these items from young people on their way into school? What reasons could there be for school supporting young people instead in the decisions they make about accessing the knowledge society?

We can envisage there being a number of potential problems with new structures that give adults little influence over the lives of the next generation. Young people are instead at the mercy of internet providers and those who market these new technologies. In many ways, through these systems, young people are being cut free from the rest of society, from their traditional communities and support networks, from adult life and from the wisdom of the past. They are instead in a marginal world where morally 'anything goes'. This cyber-world can be a dangerous one where young people are vulnerable and open to manipulation. In addition there can be the risk of a detachment from reality, where young people live in a world of 'almost now', creating alternative realities instead of facing the challenges of the real world. This is a consequence of a capitalism where there is less and less moral constraint in the free market of the globalized world.

A strange thing happens to young people on entering most of our school buildings. These new electronic devices are removed from them, placing the control of learning school-based knowledge firmly back into the hands of the teachers in the learning institutions. There is a possible dislocation between the knowledge young people are gathering freely on the 'net' and from friends outside school, and the knowledge 'given' to them from teachers in the school institutions. But is this really what is needed for schools of the future? Is this really what young people need? Could we not envision a different kind of system where young people are in some way responsible for access to knowledge? The responsibility of the school, of the education system, of teachers, is to support young people in the development of the skills to handle the knowledge. The educational institutions would now become responsible for facilitating the development of skills of analysis, of critical reflection – in fact exactly the skills that we would regard as being developed through the community of philosophical enquiry.

What do young people need to know before they leave school? Why? What qualities and skills will young people need for life in the globalized twenty-first century?

In many ways we are working with school structures that were constructed for the industrial age. Our present classroom system was devised during the latter part of the nineteenth century. Stephen Heppel has commented that the whole of the twentieth century has been spent perfecting this system of control and examination of knowledge acquisition that was established as being 'education' in the nineteenth-century system.

As we move further into the twenty-first century now, the key questions we must address as educationalists surely relate not only to the examination pass-rate of a school but to how we are preparing young people to live together in the global community of the future. To put it in rather stark terms, what is it exactly that is needed to ensure a future existence for humanity on earth?

Howard Gardner, writing in his book *Five Minds for the Future*, takes a look at the kinds of minds that people will need in order to thrive in future years. He goes further to say that these are the minds that we *should* cultivate – with a very insistent moral imperative. He says that the first three types of thinking are the kinds that he has been talking about for a very long time: the disciplined mind, the synthesizing mind and the creating mind. However, the last two have more to do with the human sphere: the respectful mind and the ethical mind. These combined areas of thinking are required to ensure the survival of the human species on the planet and they are areas of thinking close to the themes of this book. We would want to add that it is through the community of philosophical enquiry that these minds could be developed both in an integrated way and one that could lead to appropriate action in the light of the difficulties that lie ahead.

There are many challenges ahead. It is clear that we need to evolve new ideas of what it means to be a teacher and we need to evolve new pedagogical models for these times. These will be models where there can be a genuine opportunity for the co-construction of knowledge; where teachers more closely resemble facilitators of learning. The teacher will need to have a broad understanding of information systems and knowledge sources. She or he will become more like a partner on the human journey, guiding and challenging rather than imparting information and controlling knowledge. In this kind of system we may choose not to remove the new techno-logical devices from the young people routinely as they enter schools, instead inviting them to use the devices in new and collaborative ways. As educators facilitating learning we would want to work with these new technologies, enabling young people to enter into a collaborative relationship with their peers so that they can construct knowledge and understanding of the world around them.

What is your vision of yourself as an educator? What was your motivation for working in education? Did you want to make the world a better place in some way?

In a new curriculum we would acknowledge that there need to be different ways of thinking and learning in schools, which can equip young people for the world ahead. This will be a curriculum that can face up to the moral dilemmas that we will encounter increasingly in the next 20 years. This will be a curriculum that develops complex literacy skills – not just the basics of reading and writing, but of understanding, interpretation and critical analysis. There will be the need for complex translation skills, not just between different national languages but also between the languages of science, of literature, of ethics and the humanities. We will need a curriculum that develops communication skills, skills of collaboration and emotional and interpersonal understanding.

Conflict-resolution skills will be needed alongside these, so that there can be patient and caring dialogue about differences, where the realities of alternative ways of living can be accepted and where there can be increased understanding in a pluralist world, of the complexity of truth. In this kind of curriculum, the ability to engage in clear thinking will be essential. We will need to nurture the capacity for analytical and critical thinking as well as creative thinking, imaginative thinking and an ability to reflect deeply on the ethical consequences of actions. In these new educational situations novel solutions can be created and developed and a moral perspective can be brought into play and accounted for.

In the old ways of learning in the nineteenth and twentieth centuries we were preparing young people for a very different kind of world. In the old ways of learning young people were being prepared for working in factories, where they needed to be able to follow instructions. There was not such a necessity to think creatively. In the new globalized world there will be many uncertainties; there will be the need to develop new kinds of skills and competencies. In a world where resources are scarce and where grave injustice exists there will be the need to nurture a moral imagination and moral creativity. If we do not manage to do this we will have a violent future where nations and perhaps the whole of humanity is pitched into conflict, scrabbling for the pieces that are left from the tables of the rich and powerful. In this new world of the twenty-first century we need a population that is growing into full adult maturity, capable of seeking a moral future; a population capable of making collaborative, creative moral judgements where sometimes their own short-term interest is laid aside for the wider interest of humanity over the whole earth.

This kind of education will be intensely moral and will have a strong political dimension, but it will not be political in the sense that we want to encourage young people to take sides with one political party or the other. Rather it is the kind of political education that makes participation in envisioning and formulating a common human future a desirable, purposeful and meaningful thing to do. This is the kind of political activity that the Greeks advocated and that John Dewey regarded as an essential characteristic of a democracy.

We would argue, here, that it is only with such participatory democratic education that a truly moral society can form – one in which all are engaged in imagining, envisioning and working to bring into being. In such uncertain times as ours it is not always clear exactly which way we should go. There are conflicting messages and even sometimes conflicting moralities. However, we argue in this book that through participation in communities of philosophical enquiry, in communities of philosophical investigation, in our schools, in classrooms in corridors – everywhere and anywhere – young people can develop the skills needed to bring about another kind of shared understanding where all can flourish.

The major challenges to development of any new education system fit for the twenty-first century need to attend to four important areas:

- School leadership. What kinds of leaders and what kinds of leadership strategies will be needed to build schools for the future?
- Personalizing learning. How can schools be developed that allow for genuinely appropriate, self-motivated learning to take place for each individual student, which acknowledges the learning and global understanding that the young people bring into the schools already?
- Curriculum development: What kind of curriculum is needed in the twenty-first century?
- Student well-being: How can we ensure this for all young people?

In the rest of this chapter we present the theoretical framework that considers clearly how a secondary school that seeks to develop the philosophical life of the students and teacher community should begin by thinking first about the well-being of our young people. Various projects in the UK have shown that working philosophically and in community can support young people in their emotional development (for example, Gallions School, SEAL and so on). The community of philosophical enquiry, through supported philosophical dialogue in our classroom communities, can help young people's psychological development as they move towards maturity.

What would a school that was taking the health and well-being of the adolescent into account look like? What might a curriculum attempting to respond to the impact of mixed messages from a globalized world look like? How can the school personalize the ethical education it offers? What skills will school leaders need in order to have to achieve the above?

What is the importance of philosophy in the schools of the twenty-first century?

In 2006 the United Nations Education, Scientific and Cultural Organization (UNESCO) published an 'intersectoral strategy on philosophy'. Aiming to develop projects that worked across all three sectors of the organization, the document identified three strands of philosophical work that needed to be a priority in all countries. The big aim of this was to enable philosophy to 'contribute to the refining and renewal of the analysis of world problems and ongoing changes in all societies'. The intersectoral strategy on philosophy defined philosophy itself as a true exercise of freedom. This document was intended (a) to promote dialogue and philosophical analysis of contemporary questions, (b) to encourage the teaching of philosophy at all levels and (c) to promote and disseminate philosophical knowledge in order to make sure that philosophy is accessible to all.

There is a clear vision coming through this document. It is that by doing philosophy the populations of the world could become more thoughtful, more responsible critical thinkers who are more able to tackle the significant questions facing us all at this point in history. For example: 'How are we going to live together on the planet?' 'Are we going to modify our behaviour to prevent environmental catastrophe?' 'Are we going to be able to learn to live with our differences?'

> In which ways might philosophical thinking advance the cognitive development of the young people with whom you work?

The UNESCO document also suggests that it is the duty of philosophers and of philosophy itself to extend philosophy beyond a narrow field and in this way to enlighten all other disciplines as much as possible. Philosophy will then be able to contribute to refining and renewal of the analysis of world problems and ongoing changes in all societies. This document raises the possibility that it is through the *process* of thinking philosophically that we can grow and develop into moral beings capable of grasping the future.

In 2007, following the publication of the intersectoral strategy the previous year, a very large study of philosophical practices in education around the world was published under the title *Philosophy: A School of Freedom*. In the chapter on philosophy in the secondary school we can see that internationally there is a correlation between countries where philosophy is thriving and where democracy and freedom of thought and critical thinking are also encouraged in schools. Conversely, where there are political restrictions upon the population there will be restrictions or a ban on the teaching of philosophy. Clearly there is a connection between the teaching of philosophy and the development of moral societies where citizens are able to be open and critical in their reflection on issues of general importance.

It seems very likely that giving young people the opportunity to encounter philosophy and philosophical thinking during adolescence will be a significant moment in their lives where they can begin to reflect deeply about the big issues that are facing humanity. Philosophy has an affinity with the kinds of questions that have concerned human beings through all of history. Engaging young people with the thread of human thought should be part of a good general education.

It will be imperative for young people to have the chance to engage with these questions in new ways, which can also influence how they live their lives. We have seen how globalization is leading young people to be consumers on a scale that we have not seen before in human history. We have also seen the dangers of this for young people in terms of loosing their sense of cultural identity. Further we have seen the grave danger of the growing disparity between rich and poor and the disenfranchisement of vast numbers of young people across the globe – of wasted lives. There are many moral questions relating to this situation. We need to find ways in which we can genuinely engage teachers, as adult members of societies charged with particular responsibilities, and young people to address the questions that are arising for human beings in this world at this time. There has, of course, always been injustice in the world, and the great world religious and philosophical traditions since before the time of Plato and Aristotle have all sought, in their respective ways, to guide humanity through questions of how we should live together. What is distinctive and concerning about the present period of history is that the globalization of culture is cutting us away from any moral guidance that will have supported the growth of moral societies through time. A religion of consumerism is replacing wisdom of love and care for the other and the earth, which has served us well through our history.

> Has shopping really replaced religion in the lives of the young people we teach? Do teachers have a responsibility to help young people in the ethical decisions that affect their lives? Why?
>
> Is there a right answer to this question?

Evidence seems to be mounting to support a view that young people who have an opportunity to reflect philosophically in community with their peers will become more thoughtful and more responsible and ultimately grow into mature responsible adults who feel empowered to act in their lives. These will be the kind of adults who will not take things at face value but question the world in a similar way that Socrates challenged and questioned those around him. The question before us now is how to embed this into our education systems. To do this we need to understand the power that the process of philosophical enquiry has to help us do the work that is needed in our evolving global curriculum for education fit for the twenty-first century.

The community of philosophical enquiry and educational practice for building ethical democracies

John Dewey wrote extensively on the relationship between the development of a sound democracy rooted in ethical practice and principles and the development of the individual. For Dewey, there was a significant connection between what went on in the classroom and what was going on in the democratic ethical society. He did not mean that we should simply be teaching 'about' democracy, but that there should be participation in the deepest sense. Again he did not mean that young people would simply be joining school councils or participating on governing bodies, although we know that this can often make a great deal of difference in schools. (See the Hannam Report, http://www.csv.org.uk/Resources/Publications/The+Hannam+Report.htm.)

What Dewey had in mind was something even more subversive. This was for young people to be thinking together about the important issues relating to society and that through this shared exploration a reality for how to live life in this moment would emerge. For Dewey, the construction and maintenance of healthy democracy did not mean adopting a preordained externally moderated 'right way' to live in a way that perhaps Plato may have envisioned in his *Republic*. In fact, for Dewey, certainly later in his life, there was not necessarily any one right way to live at all. Dewey did not believe in an external absolute that we could discover through reason alone. Dewey had abandoned this kind of view when he moved from Hegelian philosophy towards a commitment to developing his model of pragmatism. At this point in the twenty-first century, where we are facing many difficult situations in terms of global social, environmental and economic structures, the uncertainty of our times requires a new kind of educational practice.

The emphasis of this book, building in part on the work of Dewey, is that by working with the community of philosophical enquiry in the secondary school curriculum, we can begin to support the formation of adolescents who are capable of becoming mature, responsible adults who will live in sustainable ways, enabling a fair future for all. We have a hunch, like Dewey, that it is in collaborative working with our peers that we can formulate ways of life that are appropriate for living in the present moment, responding to social and environmental needs – addressing problems that are before us right now and not looking to impose a solution more fitting for another period in history.

Over time, through working in the community of philosophical enquiry, young people increasingly find that they are more able to contemplate problematic situations and perceive the philosophical questions that lie behind them. Young people who have these opportunities in their classrooms and in other educational contexts in their lives will become the kind of people who can recognize the world situation as presenting important problems that concern them. In this way, the work of the enquiring community becomes immensely empowering. It can support the wider society in framing concerns into questions that can be discussed and explored by all. This pedagogical model for education is supportive of our democratic processes by empowering its citizens to contribute to increased participation in the decision-making processes, first informally and then in the structures of society itself.

Young people who have these opportunities will have learned skills of listening and taking the views of others into account. This will also have a great impact upon possible areas of conflict in a society. Young adults who can stand back and hear the views of others even if they are different from their own – who can hear and consider a view that they may completely disagree with – would not immediately enter into a conflict situation but would be able to engage in positive dialogue and move to a position where a solution that would work for the moment could evolve.

Through philosophical enquiry young people learn to self-regulate, to be patient and wait for others to finish speaking. It is a way of developing personal qualities of self-governance, of self-control. The community of philosophical enquiry gives ample opportunity not only for listening to others but also for hearing them and so for taking others' viewpoints into account while at the same time developing one's own. This is democratic practice at its best and it can facilitate a social and fully partici-patory democracy rooted in a reality of a shared ethical exploration where everyone's views are taken seriously. This is not a democracy that simply regards individual liberty and individual greed as a driving principle – it is the kind of democracy that Dewey had in mind when he wrote: 'democracy is more than a form of government; it is primarily a mode of associated living, of conjoint communicated experience'.

Many adults today seem to be waiting for solutions to be imposed from above – waiting to be told what to do in terms of protecting their environment, in terms of acting for social justice in the world. Is it not incredible that a species on the edge of catastrophe is unable to think and act in ways that can support its journey out of the difficult situation in which it finds itself?

The next step is to ask what is needed from our education systems in order to nourish creative ethical thinkers who can contribute towards building a future where there will be space for all to participate. This will be the kind of thinking young person who can handle working with a temporary solution; aware that more information may be needed to inform the next step of thinking, in order to move towards the bigger view. This is the kind of thinker who realizes that behind every question lies a myriad of other questions and that ultimately everything is connected and related. This is someone who is aware that the questions are complex and that there are no quick and easy answers.

If we are going to be able to flourish our democracies, we need educational structures that do much more than simply giving information about our voting rights, our human rights, or even children's rights. We need a system that engages young people in thinking critically about important questions on the nature of justice rather then simply informing them *about* our justice system.

We need educational structures that can engage young people in thinking carefully together about what kind of a world or country they would like to live in and then go on to give opportunities for action.

Philosophical enquiry and moral imagination

As well as facilitating the development of self-regulation and patience, a moral imagination is revealed and nourished by the kinds of thinking and investigation that take place in the community of philosophical enquiry.

The kind of educational and moral theory that the community of philosophical enquiry is based upon is strongly influenced by the work of pragmatists such as John Dewey. At a point in human history when the details of how we should behave are not precisely clear to everyone, an educational process that allows for uncertainty will be helpful. This process invites us to bring together three strong forces – the desires of the individual, the demands of communal life and the realities of the social problems that confront us. In the community of philosophical enquiry we aim to make progress with perennial questions in a collaborative way reaching some understanding of the questions and concerns facing us all.

To facilitate the community of philosophical enquiry into a truly philosophical endeavour, teachers have to translate their skills into those of a facilitator. They now have a more subtle but nonetheless vital and strategic part to play.

Understanding the way in which three or four kinds of thinking (as referred to in Chapter 1 – creative, critical caring and collaborative) work together to change and open the minds of those taking part in an investigation is central to understanding the way in which the community of philosophical enquiry contributes to the development of a moral imagination.

In the uncertainty of the opening decades of the twenty-first century it is likely to be increasingly important for schools to become educational contexts where young people can develop a moral imagination that will serve them as a compass to help navigate through the uncertain future. This context will be a place where working with their peers and having the opportunity to explore different possibilities for living, young people can begin to put their reflected thoughts into practice in their lives and begin to 'think globally but act locally'. Even if some rural places are more monocultural, with access to the internet or simply television, an awareness that people do things differently all over the world can be present. Here in shared enquiry we can envisage and unearth a shared concern for our common humanity.

Facilitating the community of philosophical enquiry to integrate complex thinking

The role of the teacher/facilitator in the community of philosophical enquiry is to create a democratic space where the important issues of the day can be investigated in a rigorous philosophical manner. This will be done by offering students the opportunity to create philosophical questions that are relevant to them. This will happen, as mentioned in earlier chapters, by students being presented with some problematic stimulus from which questions will arise.

Philosophical questions as discussed in Chapter 1 are distinguished by being timeless, relevant and controversial. Putting these questions to young people enables them to realize that each individual word will make a subtle difference to the possible interpretation of the meaning of the question. Examples of this taking place in different curricular contexts are presented in the third section of this book.

The teacher's role here changes considerably. She will become the facilitator both of philosophical investigation into the question, and also facilitator of the dialogue between the members of the community. These two things need to work well together – listening and probing the development of the concepts and yet also being aware of the dialogical progress between the people in the community. The facilitator must be philosophically humble: she does not put her own philosophical interpretations or views into the enquiry; this is not the place for the exposition of one particular philosophical theory or another. However, despite this, as discussed in earlier chapters, the facilitator will need to be acutely aware of philosophical ideas that are relevant to the immediate investigation in order to deepen the philosophical aspect of the enquiry through questioning. Doing this successfully is a very skilful piece of work and requires training and shared exploration with other facilitators. Training for facilitation is discussed in Chapter 11.

As well as being philosophically humble the teacher must be pedagogically strong. This means that all the group-work skills developed over the years can be brought into action here in the enquiry. The teacher is none the less responsible for the well-being of the community, for maintaining the attentiveness of the group and insisting on good behaviour. Various strategies will be explored in the final section of the book to support this aspect of the work.

With this combination of philosophical and pedagogical skill, teachers facilitate the development of the skills necessary for a deep understanding of the nature of current problems through a serious dialogue with their peers

The questions and the manner of the facilitation enable the students to develop stronger reasoning.

This can be undertaken by giving examples, identifying contradictions, searching for alternatives, predicting consequences, making appropriate inferences and so forth. The facilitator will be listening out for examples of different kinds of thinking and working with this to deepen the student's appreciation of the question in the particular enquiry.

We can appreciate how encouraging *critical thinking* supports the development of clear and logical thinking, which is needed for working towards a positive future. The capacities for critical thought are related to logical thinking and to a realization that actions have consequences. Through skilful facilitation of logical and clear thinking in the enquiry, the development of the cognitive skills that support critical thinking will flourish.

Facilitating critical thinking in the community of philosophical enquiry

The facilitator of the enquiry can develop the students' capacity for thinking critically by asking them follow-up questions during the enquiry such as:

What would follow from that?

Can any one think of an example when that would not be the case?

Is that always the case?

Can you think of another situation when that would also apply?

Creative thinking can support the development of new ideas and new imaginative solutions to difficult complex problems. An example of this can be when young people come into a room and declare that they have no thoughts about a particular question. However, when they have heard several points of view they find that they are beginning to have their own position on a question.

This is an example of how thinking collaboratively can have creative consequences for individuals and begin to unlock the imagination, allowing young people with previously fixed ideas to think about new possibilities for themselves and for the world.

Facilitating creative thinking in the community of philosophical enquiry

What if everyone in the world thought that … ?

What would happen if the opposite were the case?

How does the possibility raised by … contribute to your own ideas?

When young people learn to be considerate towards the other who may be different from them and towards different views in the community we would often say that *caring thinking* has begun. However, there is another interpretation of the meaning of caring thinking. Caring thinking is understood to be a kind of ethical or moral thinking, where caring about the immediate other in the community begins to be extended and generalized to a caring about the world and all who live in it; where the logical consequences of caring for those in the community of enquiry are explored and expanded. Caring thinking, understood in this way, will support the development of the social and emotional skills needed for the future. A democratic space where thinking in a caring way is encouraged and valued will be a central place in a school for a moral vision to be nurtured. This is quite different from telling young people what to do; it has much more to do with thinking things through together and taking shared responsibility where weak and strong are valued equally and conflict can be explored safely. The habits of respectfulness that are encouraged in the community of philosophical enquiry will develop further into the school environment at large.

Facilitating caring thinking in the community of philosophical enquiry

Can we think of another example that would support … 's point on this question?

Would all people in all countries agree with this point?

Can we think of an example from the world where this might not be the case?

Can we just listen to … as she has been trying to say something for a while.

Is there anyone who has not spoken yet who would like to contribute?

Sometimes in the community of philosophical enquiry it will be useful to break into small groups or pairs to give the quieter voice a chance to be heard. There will also be value in giving written tasks in which the students can share their ideas with the facilitator. In this way the facilitator can keep track of the development of all the students' thinking and encourage some to speak whose voice may not otherwise be heard.

The *collaborative thinking* that takes place in the community of philosophical enquiry supports the negotiating skills needed for the future. Students work together with their peers to explore a question and develop new ways of thinking about a particular problem. This collaboration can mean that students learn in subtle ways from their peers and leave any particular enquiry with a completely new view on the questions concerned.

Facilitating collaborative thinking in the community of philosophical enquiry

Does everyone agree with … on this point?

Who agrees/disagrees with this idea?

Can anyone think of another example to support/counter this point of view?

Remember to build on the ideas of the person who has spoken before you. When closing an enquiry, encourage students to think about someone else's contribution where it has helped develop their thinking.

Critical thinking in collaboration

In working with the critical aspect of the community of enquiry we are able to develop in the young people in our classrooms a critical and questioning view of the world that they experience around them. When we talk about 'critical thinking' in the community of philosophical enquiry we do not mean something that is negatively critical. We know that through investigation young people can come to realize that there is more to the world than the superficial version presented to them by the popular media. Through sensitive facilitation of the enquiry process they can come to question motives and challenge reasons for doing things. The facilitator of the community will model these kinds of challenges to illogical and unclear reasoning in the community of philosophical enquiry itself. Here the collaborative nature of the critical enquiry becomes very important. Young people can learn to 'see' or appreciate when reasoning is flawed and learn to point it out to their peers in the enquiry. Step by step, over a period of time, the students will begin to take on responsibility from the facilitator.

Thinking critically in a collaborative context enables the development of a kind of leap of imagination into the 'world of the other' – the others in the community. This is not solely empathy; one is not aiming to become 'sympathetic' to the view of the other. Rather, the aim is that young people hear the views of others and, in the context of the community, take it into account when revising their own viewpoints. If you like, I visit the idea of the other and experience it for myself in the investigation. (A theoretical explanation of this is discussed in detail in Ann Sharp's foreword to this book.) I can then return to my own viewpoint and reconsider it in the light of what I have heard. The view of 'the other' becomes a possibility – another way of viewing the world or understanding the particular issue that I am considering with my peers. I can no longer make a spontaneous judgement, an unreflected judgement that has no basis in reality. I am, in other words, forced to take another opinion or viewpoint seriously.

Young people tell us repeatedly that what they like about the community of enquiry is hearing the ideas of other people and reviewing their own ideas in the light of what they have heard. In reality this is how we grow and change. In the busy consumerist world of advertising there is so little opportunity for this kind of reflection. We do our young people a great service in offering this in our classrooms.

Thinking together for moral imagination

But it is when these four aspects of thinking (critical, creative, collaborative and caring) work together that we can observe the birth of a moral imagination. The community of philosophical enquiry becomes a kind of threshing mill where the essential seed of ideas can be sorted from the chaff of unsupported opinion – where our individual voices can quieten a little and begin to tune in to the voice of 'the other' and 'the others' and where the environment is rich with material needed to support the growth of new ideas connected to, but sometimes quite different from, the initial ideas. Here, the work of the caring and critical community can wisely leave some things behind, leaving for future investigations things that need more consideration.

In the collaborative community, students can be encouraged to investigate their questions and ideas together in a critical and clear manner and new understandings will emerge. New understandings of the ideas of others will emerge. This is very important for adolescents who are at an egocentric point in their lives. Through the work of the community, young people will come to appreciate the ideas of their peers in completely new ways.

Often they will never have had the chance to hear the reflected ideas of their classmates. In some other educational settings the kind of questioning that takes place is closed questioning. The teacher, however well meaning, asks a question for which there is usually already a fairly clear idea of what is the right or anticipated answer. In the community of philosophical enquiry, the questioning of the facilitator is of a different kind. The questions that the facilitator brings to the community of philosophical enquiry are probing questions designed to deepen the thinking of the young person and often also of the community as a whole.

When one asks enough questions, when one digs deep, eventually the bedrock of thinking comes close to the kinds of eternal questions that cause us ultimately to ask moral questions. At this point in our enquiries there will be a clear link between thinking that is done in a community, collaboratively and with a critical capacity, and the development of a creative thinking that may have a moral dimension. Here is the intersection between critical thinking and caring thinking. Here is the place where the seed of creative moral thinking becomes a shared collaborative project. In this environment the energy can be found to envisage a future which will serve the good of all rather than just a few.

Nourishing a moral imagination to engage young people with the key issues of today

Working in a collaborative community of philosophical enquiry will support the creativity that is needed for the development of the imagination – a moral imagination. This can be encouraged by giving young people the opportunity to work in a space where they can reflect upon what kind of people they would like to become and what kind of a world they would hope to live in.

We also find young people become able to develop hypothetical reasoning and envisage consequences of their actions without the need to engage in practical experimentation. This development of the potential of hypothetical reasoning is crucial in the development of a moral imagination and is something that some young people find difficult. It is essential in reducing young people's risky behaviour.

It is easier to look for certainty, shutting down the process of identity development too early. We find that young people can become more comfortable with handling uncertainty in a context where they are working with their peers and, in so doing, they can entertain more possibilities and calmly consider conflicting ideas. In this place the young people themselves can unpack the effects of peer pressure. Thinking about 'what if . . . ?' is essential to imagination and essential to a full consideration of the consequences of various possible actions. It will only be when we can consider the consequences of our actions, thinking beyond the safe, secure or familiar to other options in our lives, that we become free enough and responsible enough to make choices. Others help us to make considered moral choices in our lives. For young people this will be an essential part of an holistic, moral education fit for the twenty-first century.

Part 3

Developing Opportunities for Philosophical Conversations with Young People

6 Theory into classroom practice

We have no longer a choice: either we adopt behaviours that respect sustainable development, either we stop polluting the environment, allow for renewal of natural resources and contribute to the improvement of the well-being of all, or sooner or later we sign our own death warrant. (Koïchiro Matsuura, Director-General of UNESCO)

Getting started: why introduce philosophical enquiry into the secondary school?

Koichiro Matsura sets us a challenge and gives urgency to our task as educators. He helps us to answer the key question, 'Why is it important for me to work with philosophical enquiry in my context?' As we reflect on this question the answers that start to form in our minds will allow us to mark out the first steps.

The intention of this book so far has been to suggest that if we can make opportunities for young people to gain experience in philosophical enquiry and reflection at this important age in their lives, we will bring about a new set of outcomes. It is possible that we can work towards an educational framework that nourishes the kind of imagination and courage that can change the way we live on this planet for the good of all. In this way we have come to understand that a reason for being an educator at this time in history must be a moral one. This can be a great relief for teacher and student alike and give a new focus to a school rather than one driven by the perfection of functional skills aimed at knowledge acquisition – knowledge that is fast changing and of uncertain value. These are difficult times that need radical solutions. We can see what is necessary, but having the courage to change is not easy.

When we look at the dilemmas currently facing humanity it is clear that there will be no easy solutions. More than ever it seems likely that what will be required is for each local community to work together, to think things out for itself and cooperate towards changing ways of doing things. An example of this is the 'Transition Town Movement', which encourages communities to look at all the aspects of life that the community needs in order to sustain itself and thrive. For example, it encourages them to consider how it would be possible significantly to increase resilience (to mitigate the effects of peak oil) and drastically reduce carbon emissions (to mitigate the effects of climate change). Imagine if we were deliberately to educate for a capacity to handle transition and uncertainty in our schools, making it a priority for every moment of every day.

This chapter and the following sections give good pointers for those wishing to begin developing the community of philosophical enquiry in their educational setting. If you are beginning reading this book at this point, make sure to return at some time to the end of Chapter 1 where there is a clear account of the classic structure of the community of philosophical enquiry. It will also be helpful to look at Chapter 5, where there is an exploration of good practice in the facilitation of philosophical enquiries.

What elements of the whole-school curriculum can motivate us to make a start?

There are several governmental initiatives that can be furthered and supported through the whole school by embedding the community of philosophical enquiry into educational environments:

1. There is an imperative coming from governments in the UK and around the world for schools to work towards being **sustainable schools.** (See DfCS 2008.) One way for a school to move towards becoming a sustainable school will be for there to be whole-school engagement with philosophical enquiry around these issues – for example through PSHCE lessons and in staff meetings. Most subjects could be enhanced through the community of philosophical enquiry and in these ways young people can be encouraged to reflect together on the consequences of their actions in the light of the learning that was taking place each day. In these ways philosophical enquiry can be like the yeast in the dough in a school, raising awareness of important issues in many different ways.

2. The **Every Child Matters** agenda requires that we take into account the health, safety, enjoyment and achievement of young people in every aspect of our work with them. We also need to make opportunities for young people to make positive contributions to society and for them to develop the capacities to achieve economic well-being. The community of philosophical enquiry offers a safe space for reflection and for the growth and development of one's ideas. It

also offers a safe place to receive and give critical comments on views expressed by others, which will in turn support the development of good reasoning. This can bring a new kind of confidence for the young person. For some young people there has never been an opportunity before for their views to be heard and regarded. For some young people the only ideas they have heard are those from popular magazines and TV. This work has immense value in the building of emotional resilience and self-confidence. In this way they can become more able to determine their own future and make good judgements about how to live their lives. This could be in all areas but especially those concerning personal relationships, sexuality and career plans.

3. Working with the community of philosophical enquiry can also facilitate the development of **personalized learning** across a department or whole school. This can raise young people's awareness of their own needs because regular work in the community of enquiry enables young people to become more self-aware and increasingly reflective about their own participation and relationships in their learning community. Personalized learning is about the school's response to working with diversity and, in the community of enquiry, young people gain a sense of an increasing regard for themselves and their ideas. The young people become able to accept criticism of their ideas and views and become open to change. It is at these points, where there is a willingness to change, that real learning can take place. Where attitudes are already fixed there can be no learning. The work in the community of philosophical enquiry also develops a greater capacity to look for meaning in encounters with different learning opportunities. We have already discussed the benefits of increased opportunities for meaning-making in our consideration of David Ausubel's work in Chapter 1. There are many benefits to students from personalizing learning through this approach. Philosophical enquiry brings many opportunities for the teacher really to understand how individual children think and what is important to them. Over a period of time this way of working will increase the teacher's capacity to respond to the personal learning needs of each student. The personalizing of learning requires that the teacher nurture a high level of classroom interaction, which leads to a situation where the students themselves become self-regulating and much more aware of other students in the class and not only of themselves. This is why personalized learning is not the same as individualized learning. Becoming a person, a member of the community or wider society through one's education involves interaction and dialogue with the others around you. It is about building shared meanings. This kind of work cannot be successful with an authoritarian didactic approach to classroom management. Teachers will also grow through the process of working with philosophical enquiry; they will become much more confident and will be able to 'be themselves' with students. Over time they will develop a complex repertoire of questioning skills and be more able to respond to the deep learning needs of each student in their care. As the National Strategy website suggests, 'Personalised learning is an approach to teaching and learning that stresses deep learning as an active, social process and which is explicit about learning skills, processes and strategies (such as information processing or reasoning)' (http:// nationalstrategies.standards.dcsf.gov.uk/node/83151?uc=force_uj).

4. There is a mounting body of evidence now to show that placing **learner (or student) voice** at the heart of the vision for a school will be an important factor in facilitating whole-school improvement. One clear way of acting to achieve this in a school will be to seek ways to develop

the capability of all students to voice their views clearly and confidently but with an awareness of the value of the voices of the others in the community. The impact of the community of philosophical enquiry over time will enable these attributes and attitudes to grow and flourish.

In practice, those seeking to translate philosophical enquiry into the reality of a busy classroom in an even busier secondary school will face many challenges. At this stage of schooling in most countries there can be a heavy load of prescribed curriculum material for most subjects. Students frequently work with many different teachers, experiencing many different teaching styles.

In this third section of the book we explore several different examples of practice, of how the community of philosophical enquiry can be developed within the secondary curriculum. However, it will often be the case that when we see a clear reason and benefit for students in introducing this approach there will be many different ways of moving forward.

In the next chapter we will look at practical examples of how the community of philosophical enquiry can be developed in the secondary context by first considering how it can be developed into the thinking of a single department. Where there is sufficient experience and commitment on the part of a departmental team in any subject it will be possible to embed the work of philosophical enquiry right into the fabric of the thinking that drives a department. In this situation philosophical enquiry will be incorporated directly into the work schemes, and lesson objectives will be written that allow for the uncertainty of philosophical enquiry and yet also fulfil the many different demands that we face as secondary teachers, such as official inspection criteria and other external requirements. An example of how this has been undertaken in a religious education department will serve as a model here. This model could easily be adapted to other subjects, and this is explored in Chapter 7.

Sometimes work can best start with a cross-curricular project involving teachers in different subject area who share a philosophical perspective on education. Two examples of how this could develop are given here, the first exploring how a model for education for sustainability could be developed through enquiry and another project initiated as an Enquiry School project and funded through Creative Partnerships.

Philosophical enquiry can also be built into extracurricular projects that continue over time. An example of this is explored here through a school linking project that has developed through the shared pedagogical model of the community of philosophical enquiry.

There is also discussion of how philosophical enquiry can facilitate the learning of specific cohorts of young people, for example by developing quality classroom practice for gifted and talented students and also ways in which it can support the emotional development of disaffected young people in the school.

To make progress with philosophical enquiry in the secondary classroom there are two key skills to be increasingly aware of. These are (i) developing an increased capacity for philosophical questioning and (ii) having an increased ability to recognize and identify philosophical concepts or ideas. Further, being able to distinguish between different philosophical concepts themselves and being able to clarify criteria for these concepts are closely connected skills. However, understanding the difference between the two will be important in being able to move forward all aspects of the enquiry process.

Developing philosophical questioning across the whole school

When beginning to plan the steps forward for embedding philosophical enquiry the first thing that needs to happen is the development of the capacity for questioning. The same questioning manner can be developed at any stage of the young people's school life. In the secondary context the best place to begin will be with the younger cohort. At the same time the teacher's own openness to questioning and self-reflection will develop. As time goes by, the responses to the questions begin to include more sources and evolve into a more critical examination of the world.

There are many different kinds of proposals for developing questioning in school. One system used in UK schools, for example, has been Bloom's taxonomy. This offers a hierarchy of questions that develop different capacities in the students. The six-step hierarchy that Bloom and his colleagues laid out begins at the lower level of sophistication simply asking about knowledge. The strategy then suggests movement on through comprehension, application, analysis, synthesis and evaluation, which he regards as the most sophisticated level of questioning. However, this proposal has its problems, one of which is that there are differences of opinion about which would be the more important level of questioning. The hierarchy is possibly value-driven, and Bloom does not really acknowledge this; for example, who is to say that analysis is less difficult than evaluation? Although the taxonomy may be useful for teachers in helping them ascertain what the student understands and how, from the point of view of philosophical enquiry these hierarchical models do not necessarily lead to more imaginative and creative thinking. When the questioning comes from the teacher it becomes little more than an exercise and it cannot allow the young people to develop at their own pace and self-direct their progression.

For this reason we propose a kind of questioning that leads to development of enduring understanding. The kind of questioning that comes from learning to think philosophically advances the students' motivation to develop their own outcomes. It centres on caring and critical collaboration, offering creative opportunities for the development of the imagination through dialogue and constructing new ideas together. This is the kind of questioning we would advocate spreading through different areas of the curriculum.

In a world in which it is impossible to predict what skills and what new uses of information technology children will have access to as adults, it is not the responses to closed or hierarchical questioning from teachers that will offer students the skills necessary to succeed and thrive in the twenty-first century. Rather we look for deep, reflected, shared exploration of questions that arise from problematic situations, which students explore with their peers at their own pace, challenged by excellent facilitation to find new ways forward.

Working with concepts and criteria

When seeking to facilitate philosophical work with young people in the classroom, it will be helpful for the teacher/facilitator to be able to support them in their understanding of the key concepts under consideration at any one time. A concept is a big idea that needs to be pulled apart in order to be understood for full appreciation of its meaning. Examples of concepts would be justice, friendship, love and equality. There are concepts or big ideas relevant to each subject area in the curriculum and this will be discussed in the following chapter.

It would be possible to devise whole-class, group or paired activities to support concept clarification in or outside an enquiry. It is important to remember that not all of the philosophical investigation needs to be undertaken in the circle. There may be important points of information or clarification that can be undertaken in different ways, for example through research homework or an investigation in class on the internet.

Concept-clarification exercise

Let's take a look at a practical example of concept clarification. Suppose a question such as this were to arise: 'Does science mean that there is no point to religion?'

An important facilitation move during an early part of the enquiry would be to invite the students to think about which words need to be discussed and what meanings need to be clarified first. After a while they will become good at suggesting and understanding that it will be necessary for the group to take a look at the meaning of words. In other words it will be important to identify the key concepts in the question and to clarify their meaning before progress can be made with the investigation. The facilitator can check back with the group: 'So do we all agree that this is what we are meaning here when we use the word "science"?' Another move would be to invite the students to mind-map the key concepts with friends in a paired or group exercise, prior to feeding back into the whole group.

Another philosophical question that could arise in the enquiry might be: 'Are people more important than trees?' A key part of this question is the phrase 'more important than'. The community working with this question would need to have some criteria for making judgements about what would count as more important. How could we possibly decide this? What would it depend upon? Before working with the question, and while doing so, begin to build criteria, or a list of qualifying statements that would inform the judgement. For example, such a list of criteria could include ' better than', 'more useful than … ' and so on, until the group felt that there were sufficient to build understanding for everyone in that community.

The all-encompassing nature of a curriculum developed around philosophical enquiry will lend itself to the further development of teacher understanding. Soon, teachers will be able to build significant philosophical meaning into lessons.

Concept clarification is an unfolding process

- It is a process developing philosophical conceptualization.
- It is a process advancing skills of logical, hypothetical and inferential reasoning. ('Does it always follow that … ?' 'What if … ?' 'Could you give an example … ?' 'If … is true then what follows?'
- It will advance the development of a moral imagination by helping young people to become more open to taking responsibility for their own thinking. They will be in a position to examine their own ideas alongside the ideas of others, and to determine means of making philosophical judgements.

Essential questions for educators in the twenty-first century

A young person growing up to be a reflective thinker, able to handle difficult information and new kinds of relationships in the coming years, will need to be able to be flexible and imaginative. Some essential questions for the twenty-first century educator and learner alike will include:

- How do you know information is true?

- How do you communicate effectively?
- What does it mean to be a global citizen?
- How do I learn best?
- How can we be safe?
- How can I protect future generations?

These questions require thinking, critically evaluating, analysing and communicating. They emphasize the value of responsible behaviour and knowing yourself as an educator and as a learner. They include the way people handle technology and information. If experimentation and data analysis is a way to know something then you will have to learn how to use the technology needed to analyse data. If being safe is valued, then learning about the responsible use of social networking sites and moral issues of privacy will be essential.

Teachers believe that they can teach effective communication. The authors of this book maintain that communication and interhuman understanding without a moral imagination and without the ability to reflect and imagine consequences will be dangerous. Our capacity to link the emotional and the cognitive, to discover moral ways of behaving from our political necessities, is what makes us social and ultimately *human* beings.

The *way* we work with the essential questions of our time will be the measure of our humanity. In the context of education this will be the way we develop higher-order thinking skills, and it is fundamental for integrating values into the context of global citizenship. These are the skills that students need to achieve educationally, and they are also skills that will serve them well once they leave the arena of formal education.

What literacy skills are developed through the community of philosophical enquiry?

As discussed earlier, working in the community of philosophical enquiry will give opportunities for the development of skills necessary for broad-based literacy. This is not just about reading printed text but about knowing how to access relevant information to be able to respond to questions raised in the enquiry. Questioning skills developed through time working within the community will lead to strong enquiry skills where students know how to problematize questions or puzzles that occur in their lives. However, the risk for teachers is that young people will no longer be sponges for information that we may try to pump into them. They will become questioning and challenging.

The community of enquiry supports the development of *information-handling skills*. For example when working with the questions with the teacher, reflective questioning skills will develop that can facilitate development of skills in data handling. During the enquiry itself students will need to ask questions relating to the origin of the information:

1. How do I know whether this information is true?
2. How does this information help me become a more responsible human being?

A new curriculum, which will help young people develop a moral imagination for life in the twenty-first century will be one that allows all educators to reflect upon the way in which the young experience the world. It will, for example, seek to balance the narrow consumerist view brought to young people by the regular media. It will be a curriculum that begins to set positive patterns for young people, modelling ways in which they may continue to learn throughout their lives. For this reason such a curriculum must highlight skills that cultivate critical, collaborative and caring thinking and advance the kind of sensibilities that support the development of a mature, responsible person.

The future is of great importance, of course; however, adolescents are living in the present. For this reason we must also support them in their development of a certain courage and confidence to live their lives differently right now. Thus there needs to be a moral dimension to the whole curriculum, which is underpinned by a sense that how we live makes a difference and matters. Various curriculum statements have indicated the importance of bringing awareness into behaviour now as well as preparing for the future. We must nourish in the young person skills of collaboration, clear communication and knowledge about the affairs of the world. Furthermore, for the well-being of future generations we need a generation now that understands the impact of its actions and can appreciate the causal relationships between actions in one place and events in the lives of others in other places in the world.

Earlier in this book we emphasized that the heart of the role of the teacher cannot be the imparting of knowledge. In an information age we know that young people in our schools right now will have as much access to knowledge as we do. What they may be lacking is the ability to discern and assimilate knowledge that is worth exploring further.

In a school setting there is a key advantage of the possibility of working with others to *co-construct knowledge with clear judgement in order to advance personal meaning*. In the community of philosophical enquiry there can be a construction of new insights that is not possible on one's own. In the community of philosophical enquiry a high level of interpersonal skill is developed and a deeper understanding of the global community is facilitated.

The community of philosophical enquiry can facilitate the development of a deep kind of literacy. This is a literacy that goes beyond simply being able to read the printed text – a literacy concerned with being able to hear and understand the voices and the ways of being of others who are different from oneself. This kind of literacy can lead those involved to become able to accept and even to become interested to know more about the multitude of different ways of being amongst humanity. In this way working in the community of enquiry over a period of time can support those involved to move way beyond the simple tolerance of other ways of being towards being open to the possibility of creative and imaginative engagement with those who think differently about their ways of living.

How to write the community of philosophical enquiry into a scheme of work

When writing a scheme of work that will include lessons of philosophical enquiry it will be important to think carefully about the objectives and intended outcomes of each lesson. It can be argued that, by their nature, philosophical enquiry lessons need to have flexible outcomes in terms of knowledge, but it will be important to note that the outcomes in terms of skills and capabilities can be built up strategically over a period of time. If the teachers have a good sense of what they would like to develop in the community then they can work carefully to ensure that these capabilities are progressively acquired by the students in any particular community.

In new curricula evolving throughout the world right now there is an increasing focus on key concepts and processes. It will be helpful to look at the key concepts appearing in any particular subject area and consider how to integrate these into new schemes of work. This is discussed more fully in the following chapter.

The new emphasis being placed upon concepts is perfect for embedding the community of philosophical enquiry into the curriculum. The community of philosophical enquiry is a pedagogical model that needs clear concept development. The new curricula demand that we move away from knowledge-led planning and towards planning that is led by concepts.

The next step in medium-term planning for a term's work is to find a way to ensure that a philosophical enquiry lesson has clear learning objectives with differentiated outcomes. The work of the community of philosophical enquiry is hard work for both the teacher and the students. Lessons need careful planning and preparation; in particular the planning of developing understanding of the concepts that may arise in a particular enquiry. An example of a scheme of work written for a Religious Education course on the theme of 'the children of Abraham' is included in this chapter. The concepts being worked with are, for example, justice, hope, promises and family.

Differentiated learning outcomes

Year 7 course: The children of Abraham

By the end of this unit:

All students

- will be able to describe how Judaism and Islam are related through Abraham
- will be able to identify places in the world today where there is conflict that has a historical or religious origin.
- will be able to express in the community of philosophical enquiry something dealing with difference
- will be able to identify why the Prophet Muhammad (*pbuh*) and prayer five times each day are important for all Muslims
- will be able to describe the meaning of key words: Qur'an, Hajj and Ihram.

Most students

- will understand that some tensions in for example Jerusalem today, have their origins in conflicting beliefs about Abraham and God
- will understand and begin to be able to explain why the Prophet Muhammad and the Holy Qur'an are important for Muslims today
- will understand why prayer and Ihram are an important part of the Hajj for Muslims
- will be able to express their own opinion, supported with reasons, about whether people should be able to dress how they wish.

Some students

- will be able to explain clearly, with reasons supported with evidence from others' experience, their views on whether people should be able to dress how they wish

- will be able to explain why there are religious tensions in Jerusalem today
- will be able to interpret the evidence and express their own views supported with good reasons about current conflict in Jerusalem.

Developing lessons that embed the community of philosophical enquiry

The following page gives an example of the next step. Here a sequence of two lessons has been developed with differentiated learning outcomes. Appendix 3 gives an entire 12-week scheme for a Year 9 topic on science and religion.

Table 6.1 First two lessons in Year 7 scheme of work illustrating embedding the community of philosophical enquiry

Lesson	Key words, concepts, skills, attitudes	Intended learning outcomes AT1 and AT2	Methods, resources and homework K/V/A	Cross-curricular links: literacy/ citizenship/ PSHE	Assessment National Curriculum level
1	Analysis (investigative thinking skill)

Respect (transferable thinking skill)

Listening (transferable thinking skill)

Difference (concept)

Judgement (concept)

Fairness (concept) | **Lesson title: an introduction to difference in perception**
All students will participate in generating philosophical questions exploring how different people can experience the same situation but perceive something differently (AT2).
Most students will participate fully in the selection of the best question and engage with the key area of concern.
Most students will be able to give good reasons why they consider a particular question is the best for the enquiry.
Some students will be able to compare questions, to explain in more detail why one is better offering analysis of their views. | **Storybook**: for example 'A Walk in the Park' (A).
Generate philosophical questions for the community of philosophical enquiry. (Students all write on the board (K/V).)
Field of enquiry/area of concern introduces students to considering how two people, or groups of people, can view the same situation quite differently. Students write all questions in their books.
Choose question for enquiry next week

HOMEWORK: Students reflect on the question they think would be the best for enquiry, giving good reasons. Writing frame available. | Citizenship: exploring difference. | Teacher observes development of listening in teacher–class enquiry journal.

Teacher observation of student participation.

Written homework assessed according to National Curriculum levels. Base-line level. |

Table 6.1 continued

Lesson	Key words, concepts, skills, attitudes	Intended learning outcomes AT1 and AT2	Methods, resources and homework K/V/A	Cross-curricular links: literacy/ citizenship/ PSHE	Assessment National Curriculum level
2	As above plus self-understanding through self-regulating in the enquiry (transferable thinking skill)	**Lesson title: Enquiry on differences of perception.** **All students** will participate in the enquiry by listening and thinking. **All students** will be able to develop a first hypothesis about the chosen question by writing in books: 'At the beginning of this enquiry I think … because … ' **Most students** will contribute orally to the enquiry individually or in small groups. **Most students** will be able to *understand* what took place in the enquiry to help them make *progress* with their thinking about the question by writing, 'At the end of this enquiry I think … because … A contribution that helped my thinking was … because … ' **Some students** will be able to analyse moves made in the enquiry that allowed for progression with the question.	**Community of philosophical enquiry.** (A/K) **Desks arranged** so the group sits in a circle. **If not already done, students select a question for enquiry.** **Students building on prior philosophical skills.** **Experienced teacher carefully facilitates the enquiry encouraging students to *build on each others' ideas.*** **HOMEWORK:** Students develop written piece at home showing their understanding of the development of their thinking about the question. Writing frame available.	Citizenship: exploring difference. Literacy: written homework.	Teacher observes development of listening in teacher–class enquiry notebook. Teacher observation of student participation. Student evaluation of enquiry using the 'myself as a thinker' sheet.

Evaluating thinking-skills development through the community of philosophical enquiry

Since the late 1970s there has been much discussion about the development of thinking skills in education. As mentioned earlier, the P4C programme as envisaged by Matthew Lipman was originally conceived as a thinking-skills programme. However, we know now that philosophical enquiry in the classroom can offer more to young people today than simply developing isolated skills for thinking. It can bring together young people's thinking in a context where it can be applied to their everyday lives. Thus it offers a chance to develop moral reasoning and assist young people in their development into mature responsible adulthood.

The community of philosophical enquiry looks for and develops many different types of thinking skills. One version of this is set out in Appendix 2. In Chapter 8 there is an extended discussion of the way the community of philosophical enquiry can facilitate progress with personal, learning and thinking skills (PLTS), as in the new English curriculum. In the community of philosophical enquiry thinking skills are developed hand-in-hand with each other, but it can be helpful to tease out different categories of skill to aid our understanding of the process.

- *Good reasoning skills.* First are thinking skills, which relate to the development of good reasoning such as being able to connect ideas together with good reasons and being able to make correct inferences and to detect contradictions.

- *Investigatory skills.* Secondly there are the thinking skills that enable a good investigation or enquiry to take place, such as the forming of hypothesis, looking for evidence to support a point of view, checking for assumptions, being sensitive or aware of the context of the investigation and being able to change one's mind when something shows that one's first ideas were not correct.

- *Conceptual skills.* Thirdly there are concept-formation skills. This is an important part of philosophical enquiry as for example compared to scientific enquiry. Clearly good reasoning and good enquiry skills are important in scientific enquiry, but the skills of concept formation focus us clearly in the realms of philosophy. Here we need to be able to look for criteria and to be able to detect when things are similar and when they are different from each other. For example, how exactly do the concepts of heaven and nirvana or *moksha* differ from each other (in RE) or how precisely do we distinguish between the concept of heating and combustion (science) and when exactly does a stream become a river (geography)? We can look for dictionary definitions, but when we are thinking philosophically definitions are often frustratingly unhelpful.

- *Translation skills.* The final group of thinking skills that are developed through the community of philosophical enquiry are translation skills or skills of transference. These include being able to listen, being able to make sure that everything one says is sensitive to the context of the discussion and that the young person is not simply following his or her own train of thought. This sensitivity leads the young person to become more empathic to the views of others and able to take the learning from the enquiry out into their lives.

In the community of enquiry these thinking skills are developed in harmony and in relation to each other. It is not a functional process but an organic one. The complex interconnections and combinations of these skills form the basis for building a moral imagination. It is this interworking of different kinds of thinking in a real context, while examining a question that is of relevance and of interest to the young people themselves, that makes the community of philosophical enquiry so distinct and rich a process for the times in which we live.

For example, as young people are encouraged to think hypothetically about a proposal they have made, the facilitator will suggest, 'What if such and such were the case? Would your principle apply then?' Young people can build upon the concepts that have been clarified previously and move their thinking about the matter forward. As their skills of enquiry and investigation progress they will find ideas that they never thought of before are opened to them. This kindling of the imagination is what makes the community of philosophical enquiry such a powerfully creative process.

When we are nurturing the skills of translation we can begin to help the young people to form values that will guide their lives and build towards the formation of adult identities.

But how can we know we have made progress? We do need to be able to give some accountability for this work.

Assessment and evaluation

When we work with the community of philosophical enquiry it will be important to be able to give an account to others of the work we are doing. For this reason we will want to develop some tools to assess the progress of the enquiry.

Students' self-evaluation

There will be different kinds of assessment and evaluation depending upon those for whom this is being undertaken. There will be a place for a simple evaluation at the end of each enquiry for the students to indicate whether they feel they have made progress with their thinking on the question. This can simply be done with a 'hands up if ... ' The facilitator and all the students can look and form a judgement. This kind of evaluation can be taken further if the students are asked to go home and write something about the progress they have made in their understanding. For some classes it may be possible to give the students a special book for their philosophy work. This could be called their *philosophy journal*. Here they can take their investigations further and work on their own with regard to their thinking and research into a particular problem. This will be very useful for the teacher to read and reflect upon, informing the development of practice with the community of philosophical enquiry. Various student *evaluation forms* can also be constructed for this purpose.

Teacher evaluation

Teachers can keep their own *philosophy planning and evaluation diary* of different classes' work so that they are able to reflect upon the work of different classes and develop medium-term plans and goals for a period of time. We would recommend that there should be one book for each class that the teacher/facilitator is working with. The questions and the stimulus for each enquiry can be recorded in it and this can be the *class philosophy journal*. The students can take turns to record the important points from the discussion. The class could even cover the book and make it their own. In addition to this it can be helpful for teachers/facilitators to have a book in which they work to record the planning and preparation for all their philosophical work. The important thing is that this work with philosophical enquiry merits careful planning and thought. It is not something that can just be done well 'off the cuff' – to get the most out of this work there needs to be careful planning preparation and evaluation.

Evaluating thinking

There will also sometimes be value in works to develop more quantitative evaluation and records of observations by taping the whole enquiry and analysing transcripts. To be able to make use of this detailed information we need to think carefully what progress we are seeking to evaluate.

In the community of philosophical enquiry we are looking to ensure the development of different kinds of thinking skills or capacities. In this way a checklist as in Appendix 2 can form the basis for some evaluation. Teachers might decide that there are one or two particular thinking skills they would like to focus on for a while. These then form one of the learning objectives for the lessons and can be evaluated in different ways.

It might be helpful to focus on the progress of one aspect of thinking over several enquiries, for example by using the cognitive abilities or skills or habits listed below (see Appendix 1):

- The ability to form relevant questions.
- The ability to build upon other people's ideas.
- The ability to accept someone disagreeing with you.

- The willingness to listen to others' points of view.
- The ability to show respect for others.
- The ability to give good reasons for one point of view.
- The ability to give examples and counter-examples to illustrate your point of view.
- The ability to perceive and understand underlying assumptions.
- The ability and willingness to make judgements based upon evidence.
- The awareness and confidence to address my contributions *to the whole group* and not just to the teacher or facilitator.

Appendix 1 can help a facilitator to track the progress of one student over a period of time or to track the progress of a whole class. The second version in Appendix 1 can form the basis of a self-reflection sheet for students to fix in their books.

A further idea for raising students' awareness of the cognitive habits or abilities that support the progress of philosophical enquiry is to print out student-friendly versions and laminate them for fixing on the walls of classrooms. One or two of these can be drawn to the attention of the class at the beginning of a lesson as a focus for developing this lesson.

The important thing to emphasize is that the possibilities for developing thinking through the community of philosophical enquiry are vast. Analysis and evaluation will be a complex, detailed process. Each teacher, department or school will work on finding ways to assess particular thinking skills and integrate them into planning. The fact that these things are advanced through the community of philosophical enquiry is clear.

7 Applying philosophical enquiry to specific subjects

In this chapter we explore philosophical enquiry in individual secondary curriculum subjects, beginning first with an explanation of the classical model for this process. Many new and developing curricula around the world are no longer based solely on content but are instead moving towards an approach that emphasizes key concepts and processes. This has been the case for the English national curriculum, which began to be put in place in 2008.

The sections that follow offer examples of ways in which philosophical enquiry could take place in different subject areas. Each section begins by considering a group of key philosophical concepts that are especially relevant to the particular subject and which can generate philosophical questions for the community of philosophical enquiry.

The first step will be to determine which philosophical concepts are planned for consideration in a particular sequence of lessons. Step two will be to map out each concept, exploring the detailed meanings and relationships of ideas that it evokes. This process will generate possible questions that could be asked. The teacher will then be able to investigate ways of using the questions in the class.

The structure of a Session in a community of philosophical enquiry

There are several steps that are typical of what happens in a classical community of philosophical enquiry:

1. A stimulus is offered to the students. It should be something of interest to them, which raises problems and has the potential to evoke philosophical questions.

2. The development of questions.

3. Choosing a question that will be at the heart of the dialogue in the community.

4. Engaging in dialogue and philosophical exploration of the chosen question.

5. Giving some kind of closure to the session.

6. Evaluating the session.

1. The stimulus

The stimulus is a trigger for engaging the interest of the students. It can be a film, a piece of poetry, a painting, part of a philosophical novel or a newspaper extract with an issue that is pressing and important for the students' community. It could also be a notice about an important happening in the world at that time that forces us to understand and discuss what is going on. At the present moment, for example, it could be the conflict between Israel and Palestine.

The stimulus must have the capacity to engage the students in a philosophical discussion. For this to happen it is not enough just to have a good stimulus – it is also necessary to have a facilitator of the dialogue who is able to ask the right questions in the enquiry to take the dialogue to a higher level of abstraction. The facilitator must listen carefully and be prepared to push the philosophical thinking of the group. The preparation that the facilitator has undertaken prior to the enquiry in terms of exploring and researching the philosophical concept presented in the stimulus will pay great dividends at this point.

2. The development of questions

Discussion is stimulated when there is a concern that needs to be clarified. Something, for example, that we are not sure about but want to know more – something that makes us want to go deeper into the situation and to explore all its different aspects. This is why it is convenient and very helpful to start with a question.

Questions can be developed by asking the students to form groups of three or four and to come up with one or two questions and then to write them on the board. They can also be asked to write a question on a piece of paper, individually. Then all the questions go into a basket. You can take the first five or ten, write them up on the board so the students can see them and proceed to choose one for discussion. There are many different ways of gathering the questions. The facilitator, over time, will gain in confidence with this process, and so long as we remember that it is the students themselves who must develop the questions there can be many variations on this model. Ownership and identification with the questions is an important element of this process.

3. Choosing a question

It is important that the students feel that their questions are taken into account. The most important thing to keep in mind at this stage is that questions should be chosen in a democratic manner. The most common way to do it is to read all the questions out loud first, then read them one by one and ask the students to raise a hand if they like that question. You can tell them they just have one vote, or that they can vote as many times as they wish. Again at this point there are variations possible, but especially with adolescents it is essential that the question is chosen in a democratic manner by the young people themselves.

In this way many lessons can be learned about democracy. The young people also become confident in their own ability to make judgements about the quality of the questions. If for some reason a poor question is chosen, this is fine. The students will learn from this and may avoid making the same mistake again.

Once one question has been picked, the philosophical enquiry ensues and the rest of the questions can become the agenda for the next session, or for other sessions in the future.

4. Engaging in dialogue

During this stage it is very important that the facilitator makes use of follow-up questions that allow the group to explore the issue chosen in a reflective and truly philosophical way. Pedagogically he or she has to ensure that opinions are heard and expressed. The facilitator should try to give space for everyone to have a chance to speak and also to be able to ask the ones who talk all the time to give a chance to others to express their thoughts. The facilitator also needs to weave into the discussion the variety of positions expressed and to help students construct and build on the ideas of each other. 'How does what you just said relate to what Justin said a while ago?' is an example of a follow-up question that checks for good listening, helps to give continuity to the dialogue and allows students to put themselves in the place of others. It is through these follow-up questions that the teacher or facilitator will allow for moral imagination to develop.

> **Examples of follow-up questions for the facilitator**
>
> What would it be like if everyone thought as you do?
>
> What would be the consequences of holding that way of thinking?
>
> Is that the kind of person you would want to be or to become?
>
> Is that the kind of world you would like to live in and leave for your children and grandchildren?

It is during the stage of the dialogue that the objectives of the whole enterprise of the community of philosophical enquiry are best met. It is vital that facilitators develop in themselves the capacity to take the discussion to a philosophical level. It is only at this level that reasoning skills will be practised and developed, concepts explored and refined, and values reflected upon. It will be essential for the teacher seeking to become a facilitator of a community of philosophical enquiry to seek out some good training from those who have experience in this process. The essential elements of facilitator training are discussed in Chapter 11.

5. Giving some kind of closure

When approaching the end of the session the group needs to recapitulate the main points of the discussion, trying to find out how their thoughts have changed and how they developed or were reinforced and strengthened by the experience in the community of philosophical enquiry and by their class community itself.

> **Examples of questions to close and evaluate the community of philosophical enquiry**
>
> There can be closing questions from the facilitator such as:
>
> Did my thinking change as a consequence of this experience?
>
> Did I learn anything new?
>
> Did I understand one of my classmates better after he or she participated in the discussion?
>
> Did I learn something about someone in the class that I never expected?
>
> What do I take from this experience?
>
> Am I going to do something different in my daily life as a consequence of what I learned during the discussion?

We do not talk about making conclusions because, due to the nature of the dialogue, in most cases there are likely to be few final conclusions. Nevertheless, there *should* be a better understanding of the issue discussed, or of the complexity of the situations explored. It is common to hear students say something like: 'When we began the discussion about what a friend is, I thought I had a pretty clear idea about it. Now I am not so sure. It is not as easy as I thought it was. There were things I had not considered until my classmates raised them. I leave with a lot of things to reflect upon regarding my notion of friendship.'

6. Evaluating the session

The content of the discussion and the discussion process must be given a substantive evaluation. What did we talk about and how did we talk about it?

In terms of the content of the enquiry itself, it is important that it was philosophical; this means that the issues discussed should have been controversial, that there were various possible ways of understanding them, they were difficult to define, and they were important for everyone involved. The concepts of friendship, justice, freedom, beauty, what is considered good or bad, are just some examples of these issues.

It is also important to evaluate how the students related these issues to their own experiences and to situations in their lives that are important to them. The procedural evaluation has to do with the changes that occurred through dialogue:

Did we offer relevant reasons to back up our opinions?

Did we give examples?

Did we listen to each other?

Did we build upon the ideas of others in the class?

Did we dig deep into the concepts explored or did we just stay on the surface?

Were we able to see and understand points of view different from our own?

Did we explore the underlying assumptions of what was said?

These are some of the questions that help us evaluate the process.

The six points described above constitute the typical framework that forms the steps of a community of enquiry session. However, the teacher may want to explore other activities to complement the work of the enquiry. For this she will use her strong skills as a teacher, her pedagogical skills. For example, different work could be used as a stimulus for the enquiry, and as a follow-up to the investigation students could develop some role-play from what was discussed. Other options would be to draw or paint their findings, or follow up with further research by planning a fieldtrip to a place relevant to what was discussed. These are only some of the possibilities. Flexibility and creativity are always going to be important for the successful embedding of the community of philosophical enquiry into the regular work of a subject area.

Applying philosophical enquiry in specific subjects by working on concept clarification

Developing the work of the community of philosophical enquiry in individual subject areas has been greatly facilitated by the work on new curricula which focus on thinking skills and concept analysis. Work on thinking skills is discussed in Chapter 6 and Chapter 8. In the rest of this chapter we are going to consider opportunities presented by different concepts in different subjects for philosophical investigation in the community of philosophical enquiry.

Here is a general plan for choosing a stimulus related to a particular topic in your subject area. It should work for any subject.

Choosing a stimulus for your subject and building a plan to facilitate a philosophical enquiry

1. Select a key concept.
2. Write in the centre of a piece of paper.
3. Build a concept map of other ideas, words or concepts that are associated with this concept.
4. Choose one line of investigation.
5. Build a series of possible philosophical questions that relate to that line of investigation.
6. Think about building philosophical questions relating to each of these concepts.
7. Consider resources or news items that could result in the raising of these questions.

Once you have completed the stages outlined here, some material should have emerged as being appropriate for raising questions around the concept you are looking to develop. Through this you will be able to support a growing understanding of the concept with your students through careful use of appropriate follow-up questions in the enquiry itself. Furthermore, you should also be more aware of the area or areas of philosophical concern that will be likely to arise through this enquiry. From here you may be able to develop a discussion plan which can form the heart of your lesson-planning process. A community of philosophical enquiry is not a random discussion but a carefully crafted philosophical investigation, guided by the teacher/

facilitator. It will benefit from prior thinking and planning by the teacher/facilitator so possible lines of enquiry should be thought out in advance and exercises to develop thinking in certain areas should be available if required.

Citizenship education

Various new national curriculum frameworks for citizenship offer us a helpful way to begin planning the application of philosophical enquiry to the citizenship curriculum, whether the curriculum is to be delivered as a subject in its own right in a timetabled lesson each week or whether the subject is to be delivered *through* other core curriculum subjects. By looking at the concepts that we seek to develop in citizenship we can design curricular content, plan philosophical enquiries and prepare to evaluate out students' progress with the subject through different years. This will also help us to develop models for evaluating students' understanding and progress with the concepts.

> ### Key concepts in citizenship education
>
> Democracy and justice
>
> Rights and responsibilities
>
> Identity, diversity and community

Citizenship lends itself perfectly to the work of the community of philosophical enquiry. Citizenship education seeks to address issues relating to social justice, human rights, community cohesion and global interdependence. It encourages students to challenge injustice, inequalities and discrimination. In England citizenship education aims to equip young people with the knowledge, skills and understanding to play an effective role in their future lives as members of civic society. In the UK it is considered that citizenship education is the place where young people learn about their rights, responsibilities, duties and freedoms, and about laws, justice and democracy. Citizenship education should encourage them to take an interest in topical and controversial issues and to engage in discussion and debate. Schools should encourage them to play an active role in the life of their schools, neighbourhoods, communities and wider society as active citizens. Citizenship seeks to encourage respect for different national, religious and ethnic identities and should play a part in the life of a school that has the responsibility to equip students to engage critically with the capacity to explore diverse ideas, beliefs, cultures and identities and the values we share as citizens in the UK. Through this kind of exploration it is hoped that young people will learn to take part in decision-making and different forms of action.

However, the concept of citizenship itself is controversial, particularly in pluralistic societies and in a globalized world. We would suggest that for this to be a meaningful lesson for the students, there needs to be a way for them to engage with the complexities, inconsistencies and contradictions of the concept of citizenship itself. Where better than in the community of philosophical enquiry with their peers?

The main goals of citizenship education are very close to the goals of the community of philosophical enquiry itself, as inspired by the writings of John Dewey and in particular his work *Democracy and Education*. To support a developing understanding of the philosophical concepts of democracy the teacher/facilitator may find it useful to research different concepts of democracy. Some suggested texts are included in the Further Reading list at the end of the book.

By working in the community of philosophical enquiry over a period of time, students can learn to evaluate information. From this there can be progress towards making informed, reflected judgements based upon the findings of the investigation with their peers. The community of philosophical enquiry can also become a place where students reflect, together with their peers, on the implications of certain possibilities for action. The young people can also learn to reflect on and evaluate the consequences of their actions right now and in the future. They learn to argue a case on behalf of others as well as themselves and speak out on issues of shared concern.

Citizenship education aims to prepare young people with the knowledge and skills needed for effective and democratic participation. We would suggest that to achieve this aim there needs to be a very particular kind of classroom practice going on. This kind of aim cannot be achieved through a didactic approach to classroom practice. Such an approach would probably work against the desired outcomes.

It is important to recognize that in Scotland, unlike in England, citizenship education is not seen as a something to be taught as a subject in its own right. Instead the approach being adopted in Scotland aims to advance the outcomes of citizenship education by working through the whole curriculum. In England the proposal has been to develop citizenship as a discrete subject in its own right. Only time will tell which approach is the more effective. Whichever way is chosen to advance the aims of citizenship education, it is clear that these aims will lend themselves very well to development in school through the work of the community of philosophical enquiry. This will help students to become informed, critical, active citizens who have the confidence and conviction to work collaboratively, take action and try to make a difference.

Examples of work suitable for community of philosophical enquiry within citizenship education for older teenagers can be found in many useful and relevant videos on YouTube (http://www.youtube.com): for example, a piece called The Story of Stuff, or another video from Jonathan Porritt on consumerism. These were produced as part of a topic on justice and rights. Questions arising from working with these concepts included:

- Should we relax and enjoy our lives, or just try to earn as much money as we can?
- Should we value all the things we buy equally?
- Should we always think carefully about where what we buy is produced?
- Should everyone in the world have the right to buy the same things?

The last question was voted as the one that the community most wanted to discuss. Students engaged in an enquiry into the rights of everyone and about what responsibility the government has to ensure that everyone in a nation or the world had those rights, freedom of choice, opportunities and aspirations. The groups talked about natural resources and whether there were limitations on the resources. Although students did not convince each other, they were able to listen and accept different views and challenge the reasons that others were giving for their views in order to begin to ascertain which reasons were better justified.

Making some kind of evaluation is important, as we have discussed. And in this case it was also important to clarify whether students were able to notice the progression they had made with their investigation. For educators, it is also important to be able to explore what the impact has on the students as a result of work with the community of philosophical enquiry.

At the end of several weeks a plenary can be held to discuss with students what they feel about their community of philosophical enquiry.

Student evaluation of the community of philosophical enquiry

- I feel that people listen to me now.
- I feel that I can say what I think and know that I will not be ignored.
- I didn't realize that my ideas and opinions were any good, so I didn't speak before.
- My opinions matter, but they're not always right.
- I realize that I wasn't listening to other people and now I do much more.
- It helps me to clarify my thinking when someone disagrees with me.
- People who never say anything in other lessons talk here so we know what they think.

- I feel that I will not be afraid to discuss things with adults in the future because I know I have ideas and views that they can listen to.
- I think about what I want to say more now instead of just saying anything.
- We should think about things, not just sit and listen because in this lesson I learned to value the ideas of everyone through thinking carefully.

The community of philosophical enquiry supports the work of the key processes of critical thinking and enquiry as well as advocacy and representation.

Design and technology

Throughout human history we have been engaged in the process of making things to advantage our lives in some way. Although apes have been recorded as using simple tools it would seem that working with complex tools and making things for both practical and purely aesthetic use is one of the distinguishing features of our humanity. In design and technology in the secondary school young people develop practical and technological skills in combination with creative thinking to design and make products and systems that meet present human needs. They need to be able to think imaginatively about the future and consider the impact of future technological opportunities on the life of human beings. Students learn to think creatively and to reflect on their interventions in order to improve their quality of life, solving problems as individuals and members of a team.

From our reflections in this book on the issues surrounding globalization we know that bringing a moral imagination into the work of technology and design is imperative. The opportunity for philosophical enquiry in design and technology will bear much fruit.

Key concepts in design and technology

- Designing
- Making
- Cultural
- Creativity
- Critical evaluation

When considering opening up a space for philosophical enquiry in design technology subjects it will first be helpful to think about how important supporting work in a collaborative atmosphere is for designers. Frequently design is something that happens in teams; all the more reason for young people to have the opportunity to work collaboratively in the community of enquiry. When working with the concept of design in a community of philosophical enquiry young people will come to understand that designing and making have aesthetic, environmental, technical, economic, ethical and social dimensions. These are all ideas worthy of philosophical investigation. Nothing in the present climate is a given any longer. Students need to think about the way in which their designing will impact on the wider world and also about the sustainability of their work. Through philosophical enquiry students can integrate their learning and understanding from other subject areas about how different ethnic perception and religious beliefs influence design and technological developments.

A central concept in design and technology subjects is that of creativity. In this area reasoning and enquiry skills developed in the community of enquiry support creative and imaginative thinking in the context of design. Students have the opportunity to interpret and apply learning in new contexts and can share and communicate their ideas in new or unexpected ways. Students have the opportunity to explore and experiment with the complexity of ideas, materials, new and old technologies, the variety of techniques available. An important part of the design process is, of course, the analysis and evaluation at the end of the production stage. Analytical and critical thinking skills developed through the process of the community of philosophical enquiry will be of immense value.

English

There are of course at least two crucial elements to the teaching of English: literature and language. The community of philosophical enquiry would lend itself well to both parts of this subject as both need students to bring a balance of the critical and the creative aspects of thinking and writing to the subject.

English is a very concise language. A key area of concern is to engage students in a discussion of the importance of expressing oneself clearly and accurately, both orally and in writing. Students will find it interesting to explore the reasons behind seeking to be accurate in punctuation and spelling, for example, and even to consider whether these rules could be different.

Literary criticism is very close to philosophical investigation or enquiry. Understanding and appreciating the motivation for people seeking to express the most profound, the most sublime and beautiful elements of their experience through literature or through poetry is an investigation which belongs very well in the community of philosophical enquiry.

The key difference in this approach is the way that teachers see themselves in the classroom. Rather than leading a discussion or sharing with students the understandings of others on these matters, the teacher has to step back and facilitate the students' own exploration of these engaging questions of grave and constant human concern.

Key concepts in English

Competence – being clear and concise in expressing oneself will be an important and interesting philosophical concept to explore in English

Creativity

Culture and understanding culture

Critical understanding

Geography

Many new curriculum frameworks being developed for geography now require that the key processes in geography facilitate the growth of students' capability to ask geographical questions and that they should be 'thinking critically, constructively and creatively'.

Probably some of the more engaging geographical questions are in fact philosophical questions. This means that they are the kinds of questions for which the answer is uncertain and are of perennial human interest. They will probably be the kinds of questions that have an ethical dimension to them.

In working with young people in a geography classroom we will be intending to develop a capacity for students to think like geographers. One of these skills will to be able to engage in geographical enquiry or geographical investigation. In a geographical enquiry students need to be able to formulate a hypothesis and test this hypothesis to form and re-form new theory. These are exactly the skills that can be learned with ease through the community of philosophical enquiry.

> **Key geographical concepts**
>
> Scale
>
> Interdependence
>
> Physical change in the environment
>
> Human impact on the environment
>
> Sustainable development
>
> Culture
>
> Diversity

A similar process to that discussed above can be used to begin to develop the community of philosophical enquiry into geography. Take one of the key concepts that are being used in a particular topic of study and map and expand it. Follow a train of investigation and then begin to think of the kinds of philosophical questions that could arise from this aspect of the concept. From this reflect upon what could be a good stimulus for opening up this problematic area with students. At this point it is possible of course to choose a stimulus for opening the questions that is age and in other ways appropriate for the students with whom you are working.

Choosing a stimulus in geography

One of the greatest challenges for many geography teachers is to encourage young people to apply the skills they are developing to real life situations. The problem could be helped if young people were encouraged to develop their own questions and in so doing begin to apply their skills.

Geographical questions are often described as being in one of two groups:

- questions that can be answered by access to primary data alone, such as things that can be counted

- questions that need additional secondary data to further and extend the investigation, including the use of maps, CD Rom, the internet and textbooks.

Building philosophical enquiry into the geography curriculum

We would like to propose that there is yet another kind of geographical question that cannot be addressed adequately by accessing primary and secondary data alone. We would regard such questions as philosophical and they may often be ethical. They could relate either to physical or social geography.

Which of these geographical questions would you regard as philosophical?

Which of these could be answered by accessing primary data alone?

Which of these could be answered by accessing primary and secondary data alone?

Which of these questions would benefit from a philosophical investigation?

How many shops are there in my high street?

What other shops do we need in my high street?

Where are the flood defences in the UK?

Should there be more flood defences in the UK?

What is the cause of the increase in global flooding?

Are there too many people in the world?

Is there a relationship between deforestation and global trade in timber products?

Is there a relationship between deforestation and agricultural policy?

Should everyone have access to water from a tap?

Why do people live near areas of seismic activity?

This approach, over several years, could lead to the creation of confident geographers who are ready to take on the world with a critical and ethical eye, ready for the twenty-first-century problems that they will have to face. How better to help young people begin to apply their skills of geography into real-life situations than to allow them to bring their real lives into the classroom for analysis and discussion with their peers?

There is vast scope for working with the community of philosophical enquiry in geography. With new initiatives on education for sustainable development, the opportunities for investigative thinking are expanding.

History

The acquisition of confident questioning skills is a very important factor in the development of strong historians. The ability to recognize and identify different kinds of historical questions and also to use evidence to support hypotheses is essential in order to achieve higher levels of historical understanding.

History is not fixed. Knowing and understanding the precise course of events in any one period of time is extremely hard. History requires high levels of interpretative understanding. These and other important historical skills can be developed well through working in the community of philosophical enquiry. Examining the key concepts in this subject is, as is often the case, a very useful way to begin.

Key concepts in history

Time and chronological sequence of events

Cultural, ethnic and religious diversity

Change and continuity

Cause and consequence

Judgement about significance of events

Interpretation, evaluation and analysis of events

New Zealand provides a useful example to illustrate the way in which history students could benefit from philosophical enquiry. In the two societies that in many respects work alongside each other in New Zealand, European and Maori, redefining common ground while celebrating diversity raises some difficult issues about toleration. In New Zealand schools, citizenship touches on empowerment and social action as well as building knowledge about how democracy works. However, there is evidence that there needs to be an understanding of other cultures at deeper levels of engagement.

When considering how to teach history in pluralistic situations, the UK could learn a great deal from New Zealand. The work there involving the Maori and Europeans can lead us to ask how non-Islamic groups in the UK can see beyond fundamentalism to the rich culture of Islam. Is it, for example, possible to develop a capacity for mutual critique? How can dialogue about identity and the reality of history be facilitated? What does it mean when Gordon Brown invites educators to consider Britishness? Has the drive to embed ideas such as human rights consciousness in school curricula compromised the need for deeper contextual understanding of important historical events like Magna Carta or the events of the First and Second World Wars: for example, Gallipoli, and Dunkirk? Can historians help curriculum planners find meaning in the vast amount of historical content that is available?

We would suggest that, given the contestable nature of history, it lends itself perfectly to the work of the community of philosophical enquiry and that the combination of thinking skills that develop as a consequence of its exploration in the community would be of immense value to the development of competent historians who are open to the thinking needed in the twenty-first century. For the teacher, this work gives space to facilitate a truly personalized curriculum in history where there is the genuine opportunity to co-construct knowledge and understanding.

Mathematics

The nature of mathematics is to be philosophical. As we know, many of the world's great philosophers – Plato, Leibniz, Descartes, Spinoza and Russell – have also been eminent mathematicians in their own right.

Several mathematics projects have taken place in the UK and elsewhere. Many find that the community of enquiry is a wonderful forum to work with. In particular it can support young people in their realization that maths is an essentially creative subject where there are many uncertainties.

Topics that are suitable for mathematical enquiries would involve issues such as probability, space, shape and number. Teachers at Ulverston Victoria High School found that philosophical enquiry was an excellent way to motivate students to have a greater interest and engagement with mathematics.

Religious education

Religious education lends itself to a questioning and philosophical approach. In a world where many international conflicts have a religious dimension we would not be serving our teenagers well if they did not leave school well informed about religious matters.

In the late 1980s many had thought that, with increasing secularization and globalization of material values, religion would have quietly died away in Europe. However, this has clearly turned out *not* to be the case. The migration of people across the world, due to economic and political reasons for example, has been followed by the movement of the faiths of those people. Developing genuine understanding of other faiths will be, without doubt, an important way of advancing community cohesion.

This is not just about increasing tolerance in society, although of course this is an important beginning. Tolerance can be superficial and if it has no basis in deeper understanding can easily slide back to intolerance. To understand the ways of life and beliefs of others will mean one has to first develop a secure understanding and appreciation of one's own beliefs and values. Religious education can help young people develop their own sense of identity and belonging and to appreciate the diversity of religious belief and culture in the world today. The National Framework for Religious Education in England and Wales and the new Scottish and English National Curricula all show the value of religious education to the well-being of individuals and society.

Problems can arise, however, when the beliefs of one religious tradition are fiercely contradicted by the beliefs of another. For a young person, trying to appreciate and make sense of this can be difficult and can lead to disbelief or cynicism in the possibility of religion contributing to human society or, for the young person from a faith community, to confusion. There has to be a way to deal with the contestable areas of a pluralistic religious education. We have seen that working with contestable problems and questions is exactly the area for philosophical investigation and enquiry. Furthermore, it can also be the case that when working in the community of philosophical enquiry in religious education lessons we can advance the skills that can enable young people to move beyond tolerance towards an understanding and appreciation of difference. Young people who have had the opportunity to experience philosophical enquiry over a period of time can work confidently with ambiguity and uncertainty.

> In a philosophical enquiry you get to hear other people's points of view. There are lots of voices in the world, and in an enquiry you get to hear some of them. I have learned to appreciate that people can think differently from me. Sometimes I might change my mind about an idea or think about something in a way I had not thought of before. (Becky, 14)

Philosophy for children is underpinned by a desire to advance what can be understood as being 'good reasoning'. This is not just logical reasoning but can also be exemplified by the collaborative reasoning and shared thinking that goes on in the community of philosophical enquiry. It is not simply being able to reason, or to be rational. Reasonableness combines sound thinking with clear conceptualization and ultimately forms people who are able to make strong ethical decisions and live well.

> ... everyone has their own say and listens and thinks more because other people are saying what they think. You can disagree and say why you think their reasons are not strong ones. It helps me to develop my own ideas and beliefs about the world. (Nathan, 14)

Working with philosophical concepts is something that we do frequently in religious education.

A community of enquiry is philosophical when the teacher/facilitator encourages students to take the enquiry deeper into the ideas raised. The teacher must be able to recognize a philosophical idea when it comes up. Religious education teachers often have a good understanding here. Philosophical concepts include justice, love, responsibility, freedom, friendship, hope, God and what it means to be human.

Philosophical enquiry can help young people form the values that will guide their lives. The community of philosophical enquiry helps students to investigate and make reasoned judgements with their peers about what kind of people they want to be and what kind of a world they want to live in.

However, in a world where there is increasing conflict over truth claims, as is clearly presented in the religious education classroom, the community of philosophical enquiry has an especially valuable part to play. See Appendix 3, which is a practical example from a GCSE unit on science and religion.

Science

The skills of enquiry and investigation lie at the heart of good science because the scientist is working with hypothesis and enquiry. The skills developed in the community of philosophical enquiry will therefore be exactly the skills that are needed by the good scientist.

The teaching of science for 11–16 year-olds has changed a great deal in recent years, making more pressing demands on the teacher to be innovative. The progress in scientific knowledge is so rapid that no teacher can have all the knowledge that could be required for any one topic. The teachers need to be importing the skills needed by a scientist and facilitating the young people to work with scientific concepts. All this is perfect for the community of philosophical enquiry. There are many similarities, after all, between philosophical enquiry and the process of scientific enquiry.

Key concepts in science

Theory

Explain and analyse

Cultural understanding

Ethical and moral implications

Collaboration

Summary

Practitioners of the community of philosophical enquiry in any subject area of the secondary school will begin by using the same kinds of strategies. First they will seek to explore the philosophical questions relating to their own subject. They will look for ways to engage students with the key questions in their subject. They will be able to recognize the concepts and ideas that are at the heart of their subject and also the kinds of concepts that facilitate the process of endeavour in their subject. For example, in science process concepts would include 'theory' or 'investigation'. A key idea or concept at the heart of science could be something like 'gas' or 'liquid'. Having identified the concepts, the next move is to seek something that could act as a stimulus for enquiry – something that will support the students in forming their questions. With the questions and the care of a facilitator – keen to support the students humbly on their journey of investigation, the endeavour of opening moral imagination fit for the twenty-first century can begin.

8 Applying philosophical enquiry in cross-curricular projects and themes

Sometimes in an informal conversation in the staffroom it transpires that a group of teachers shares an interest in philosophy, philosophical thinking in education or philosophical enquiry. Sometimes two or three staff in a school have independently accessed training in the community of philosophical enquiry through a national organization. In these cases one way to proceed with introducing philosophical enquiry into a school could be through taking a lead on a whole-school or cross-curricular initiative. This gives teachers with a shared interest in this aspect of curriculum development the opportunity both to develop their own practice as teachers and to work in this constructive way with young people.

In the examples that follow in this chapter, we consider how philosophical enquiry can be applied to aspects of a school curriculum through 'whole-school' issues and in innovative cross-curricular practice. We are concerned to build educational institutions and educational practices that will allow the flourishing of the qualities needed for the next generation to have a moral imagination sufficient to build a healthy future for us all. The three examples cited here all give opportunities to develop these qualities.

The first example of a whole-school issue considers how the community of philosophical enquiry can support the embedding of personal, learning and thinking skills (PLTS) into a curriculum. Following this is a discussion of the place of the community of philosophical enquiry in developing identification strategies, provision and policy for gifted and talented students.

Finally we consider a cross-curricular creative project bringing together religious education and citizenship, which was supported by Creative Partnerships. The National Curriculum in England encourages reflection upon key concepts across subjects to facilitate creative work. This is perfect for embedding the community of philosophical enquiry into project development, as philosophical enquiry itself uses concepts to advance philosophical thinking and reflection. In this way the project itself becomes a philosophical question about educational practice and outcomes.

This project can also serve as a model, giving a sound pedagogical foundation for embedding personal learning and thinking skills into cross-curricular projects.

Personal learning and thinking skills

The PLTS aspect of the new National Curriculum in England offers a framework to describe the skills and qualities that may be needed for life in the twentieth century. It is likely to have a great impact because of the way it is seeking to link together a more personal focus so that students can make progress with the skills needed to live well in the twenty-first century. It is not advocating individualism or an individualistic approach to learning but something softer; it is a way of advancing students' own understanding of their learning needs and also their needs as human beings growing up in local and national communities and in a globalized world. The kinds of things that are involved include developing awareness of others and developing the need to listen carefully to each other and to be able to work together.

The PLTS skills work of the school will link closely with the way the Every Child Matters agenda is developed into a school's planning. There is evidence that behaviour is improved through the work of the community of philosophical enquiry and where the three things can be woven together in a school an integrated vision for well-being and behaviour can be developed. We have discussed the role that the community of philosophical enquiry can play in the development of adolescent identity. It is clear then that where a holistic view of the way young people are included in their education can be advanced and philosophical enquiry is seen as a key to this, even the most disaffected young people can be brought into the life of the whole-school community.

The framework for PLTS includes six groups or clusters of thinking skills: independent enquirers, creative thinkers, reflective learners, team workers, self-managers and effective participants. Each cluster of skills is dependent on and related to others. Each can be facilitated through the community of philosophical enquiry.

Examples of measurable impact of developing PLTS through the community of philosophical enquiry

- *Independent enquirers.* The community of philosophical enquiry can support students in becoming independent enquirers by enabling them to develop advanced questioning skills.
- *Creative thinkers.* The community of philosophical enquiry can support students in becoming creative thinkers by helping them generate their own ideas and think about the consequences.

Students learn to connect their ideas with the ideas of others and develop advanced skills to question assumptions.

- *Reflective learners.* The community of philosophical enquiry can support students in becoming reflective learners by helping them to become confident in giving and receiving critical comments on their ideas. The enquiry space also gives opportunities for students to reflect upon their own thinking.

- *Team workers.* The community of philosophical enquiry can support students in becoming team workers by encouraging collaborative thinking in the community with their peers. Here students learn to build upon each other's ideas and to recognize the contribution that all the students in their class have to offer in developing an idea or exploring a puzzling question carefully.

- *Self-managers.* The community of philosophical enquiry can support students in becoming self-managers by helping them to learn to be self-regulating in terms of their behaviour and listening in the community. Here the teacher takes on a new role of facilitator rather than leader or expert. In this way students learn to be self-managers rather than looking continually to the teacher for control and guidance; they begin to take more creative risks with their thinking and planning and so develop their capacity to think about and plan their work independently.

- *Effective participants.* The community of philosophical enquiry can support students in becoming effective participants, as they gradually learn that their contributions are regarded and valued. They take on a share of the responsibility for the well-being of everyone in the community of enquiry. Students see the consequences of their actions, and this is the first step towards acting responsibly in the community of the school. Where philosophical enquiry is introduced into guidance lessons students can support each other in taking on new challenges in their school and wider community.

In many respects the PLTS skills are exactly those that are nourished through working with the community of philosophical enquiry over an extended period of time.

The framework is helpful in making the links between thinking itself and assessment for learning. It offers a possibility or model for assessing when the skills have been developed. However, a narrow evaluative model alone cannot offer a practical plan for actually developing these skills in students' lives. We would suggest that it is necessary to acknowledge the difficulty of dealing with thinking and personal development in a functional way. A pedagogical model such as the community of philosophical enquiry offers a strong comprehensive framework that has sufficient complexity and theoretical background to support the embedding of PLTS into the whole school. The table in Appendix 2 shows how thinking skills that are developed in the community of philosophical enquiry can be helpfully set into four types of skill. Mapping this against a particular thinking-skills frame such as PLTS can help the facilitator form a good idea of the skills that he or she is looking to nurture in a particular philosophical community.

Human beings from birth to the age of 5 are quite good at learning to think, given a rich environment where adults talk and offer creative opportunities for children's thinking and speech development, which of course go hand-in-hand. However, in schools the curriculum is too often narrowly defined in terms of closed subject boundaries. Creative thinking is not restricted by subject boundaries and to develop the skills needed for the twenty-first century schools need to give space for bridges to be formed between subjects. In this way, learning becomes a genuinely collaborative project where knowledge is co-constructed. When students are regularly involved in this process through classroom enquiry and investigation they will begin to see through the boundaries between subjects, and collaborative and truly creative learning opportunities will open up.

In the work of the community of philosophical enquiry students are given the opportunity, through a facilitated philosophical conversation, to think creatively and imaginatively and yet critically with others. The PLTS framework enables students to acknowledge these skills with their peers and encourages them to transfer the skills learned through the community of philosophical enquiry to other subject areas.

The PLTS framework can also become a helpful way of assessing progress in the community of philosophical enquiry and for students to assess how they are transferring these skills into their wider school life. A booklet could be created with the skills clusters as defined by the PLTS framework; students can then use this to support their reflection and evaluation of their understanding of the suggested skills. It would be possible to use this to develop evaluation tools for the community of enquiry.

Thinking, however, cannot be undertaken in a vacuum; it must be part of the nurture and development of the whole child through adolescence and on into adulthood. For a responsible future, these thinking skills need to be contextualized and rooted in a moral framework. This is where working with the community of philosophical enquiry has a distinct advantage over other thinking-skills programmes. When young people are working with their peers in the community of philosophical enquiry, their investigation is placed in a context that is relevant and interesting to them rather than being imposed from the outside. The questions that young people work with are those that they have chosen themselves and not those chosen by the teacher. The teacher's skill is to facilitate the enquiry in a way that develops the thinking skills.

The cognitive skills that develop in the community of enquiry as listed in Appendix 1 have a strong relation to the PLTS framework and can act as a initial way for teachers to introduce the desirable cognitive and behavioural skills that help a community of philosophical enquiry grow over time. Highlighting these features to students will support the eventual development of their thinking skills and can later be developed into a cross-curricular approach to PLTS. When a school begins to reflect upon how it will work with PLTS, the community of philosophical enquiry should be considered as an integrated way of managing the task of advancing thinking, learning and personal skills of all students in the school.

The community of philosophical enquiry and work with more able young people

It is probable that for many years children's and young people's capacity to learn, to think and consider life from a moral perspective has been underestimated. This would be as true for the general community as for the more able or gifted young people in our schools. The teaching of logical and critical thinking skills has been more or less absent in our school systems until quite recently. The connection between developing a global, social and moral awareness and the work of these logical skills has been overlooked. In order to think clearly, young people, and particularly gifted young people, need to be given opportunities to explore and be challenged in their thinking in order to develop the capacity to handle the complexity of higher-order thinking skills in context. The community of philosophical enquiry, when developed carefully into programmes for gifted students, can be a space where their critical thinking skills are developed, giving opportunities where they can apply their higher reasoning capabilities in the context of real-life examples in the questions they have chosen.

For some in mainstream schools the concept of 'giftedness' or being 'more able' imply qualities or capacities that are given at birth and fixed once and for all. For those who work from this basis, developing the gifted child involves offering 'enriching experiences' that, for a select group of students, somehow develop them so that they can achieve A** grades.

However, giftedness is not necessarily fixed at birth; rather, it is something that needs to be cultivated and revealed. There is often the potential to co-construct the qualities that we would regard as being more advanced and perhaps more intellectually skilled. This concept of giftedness would include a growing moral awareness and understanding. A truly gifted young person is one who has a rounded perception of the way things are in the world and also has the personal qualities to act in the world in positive and caring ways. The view of giftedness presented here is one that seeks to move away from a narrow cognitive perception that overemphasizes rationality at the expense of other human characteristics (see for example Balchin et al. 2008). The model of giftedness we are working with here would suggest that a school that is seeking to serve the whole child will be making provision that gives the opportunity for global, social, economic and environmental issues to be considered. The capacity for moral imagination in students working at a high level of intellectual challenge is immense. For these students the possibility of integrating their thinking in a collaborative, critical but caring environment will prove to be greatly satisfying both intellectually and emotionally.

One of the best ways to facilitate the development of giftedness, we would suggest, is through the practical work of the community of philosophical enquiry. In the community of philosophical enquiry we can see the development of a range of skills and habits of thinking and acting, as has been discussed earlier in this book (see p. 9).

From our experience of working with the community of philosophical enquiry we see that critical and caring thinking work together; there is a kind of symbiosis and one is lacking without the other. Through guided philosophical investigations students are encouraged to develop their capacity for critical and logical thinking, for example by gaining expertise in hypothetical reasoning (What if … ? If such and such were the case then it would follow that …). Over time, being progressively open to the thoughts and ideas of others can be lead to increased care and concern for 'the other'. In the community of enquiry students who may already have advanced cognitive abilities now have an opportunity to develop their capacity to care and consider the implications for their actions and hear the views of others on the same topic. In this way an increasing emotional literacy develops alongside a greater capacity for patience, together with a growing awareness of the need to take the views of others into account.

When working with a closed concept of giftedness there is always a possibility of the 'gifted' child becoming arrogant or even complacent. Where children are told repeatedly that they are bright they can relax and not consider the other sufficiently. Sometimes they can begin to rest on their laurels and even cease to make the commitment to pursue their academic progress. At this point a school would be likely to make interventions of many kinds. We can be reminded of the story of the hare and the tortoise, an image that Guy Claxton has developed most thoughtfully in his book *Hare Brain, Tortoise Mind*. Sometimes the children who presented at primary school as being 'bright' do not achieve in the way that was hoped by the time they are 16. Sometimes it is the students who have a greater emotional resilience are the ones who actually achieve, and the teachers of those students who seemed bright are completely perplexed. Claxton and Meadows (in Balchin et al. 2008) invite us to remember that concepts such as giftedness are 'inferences and attributions, not statements of self-evident facts'. With such an understanding we can begin to perceive another way of working in schools that needs to be put in place in order to facilitate the highest and broadest understanding of what achievement would really look like in the long term for the most able students in our care.

According to Matthew Lipman, the most important thing that all students need to progress confidently, but which we suggest is even more necessary for the more able student, will be for them to have 'a questioning teacher and a group of students prepared to discuss things that really matter to them'. The teacher's role in this situation is to stimulate and facilitate the discussion and not to say what is good or bad, right or wrong. Teachers must suspend their judgement and in so doing exercise strong pedagogical skills. In such an environment all students learn to take their own views seriously and not to laugh at each other for saying things that are new and different. In such an environment, more able or gifted students can begin to try out their voice in ways that they may not otherwise have the confidence to do. Gradually the children in the classroom begin to discover that a philosophical discussion has a different style from any other type of discussion. It's not just a matter of getting things off their chest or being able to indulge in self-expression. They begin to experience and come to value each other's different viewpoints and look at them with a critical but caring eye. For the gifted child, this may mean that they will come to recognize that the contribution of a child they had previously pigeon-holed as being 'stupid' or 'not clever' has value and that this child that has something to teach them which they had not thought of before. This is how caring thinking emerges from collaborative thinking. It is the beginning of a great shift in personal awareness that has to take place if the more able child is to have the vision for a different, more just world, where moral imagination fit for the future can flourish. It may be uncomfortable for more able children to realize they have much to learn from someone they had up until now boxed into a less valuable position. However, it is in this kind of uncomfortable zone, as Vygotsky reminds us (Chambliss 1996), that we make the most strides in our learning.

In this kind of environment more able or gifted students will experience the satisfaction of connecting up different aspects of their learning from within the school and connecting with the extensive learning that they will be doing outside school. For perhaps the first time they will be freed up to acknowledge and have acknowledged their wider visionary thinking, because the process of acceptance works in both directions in the community of enquiry – it is both given and received. Here students otherwise labelled as 'geeks' can share their understandings and receive positive regard from all their peers.

In the community of philosophical enquiry they can gradually acquire an increased sense of the value of others and of others' views. This can be a spur for more able students to reflect on new ways that they had not thought about before. They may find that they need to think through new problems raised in the community, which they had not previously considered, rather than being satisfied with their own independent discoveries. It is at this point that the more able or gifted students will develop new ways of thinking and continue to learn with great long-term advantage for all.

'Enquiry school' project

The 'enquiry school' project run by Creative Partnerships in the UK involved working with an artist across two subject areas,. The programme aimed to work with schools over a period of one year, exploring how creative teaching and learning can enhance practice. Enquiring schools involved in the scheme decide on a specific focus for their programme in relation to the broader needs of the school. In the project referred to here, the artist worked closely on the planning of the project with the RE teacher who was skilled in philosophical dialogue. Other teachers were involved in the original envisioning of the work. The project sought to ascertain how different kinds of enquiry – artistic investigation and more verbal investigation in the community of philosophical enquiry – could interconnect to support students' development of identity. This cross-curricular project involved citizenship and RE and looked to develop a deeper understanding of the relationship between more practical and conventionally creative forms of exploration and the kind of creativity expressed in the form of reasoned arguments in the context of a shared cross-curricular exploration of identity. The research question that directed the whole project and was developed by the teachers in the enquiry schools project was: 'In what ways can a cross-curricular enquiry approach to learning support KS3 students to think creatively about their sense of identity?'

Through the community of philosophical enquiry it was possible to generate questions relating both to personal and group identity. The class community had the opportunity to engage with facilitated philosophical enquiry regularly. This was an important part of the project. This enabled trust to develop in the class more quickly and allowed students to develop their enquiry and investigative skills faster than is usually the case in the secondary school.

The concept of identity occurs in Key Stage 3 key concepts for art, religious education and citizenship. By identity we mean two things:

- a personal sense of identity that can contribute to students' sense of purpose in their lives and in their educational careers;
- a sense of community identity and membership of a particular group. This could be understood by the students to be for example the school community or even their national or global identity as human beings.

The process was facilitated in the beginning by mapping shared concepts across three subjects as they appear in the English National Curriculum. Through exploration of these shared concepts we were able to develop a creative programme of study to explore students' sense of identity.

Looking for common ideas: examples of concepts across art, citizenship and religious education

A starting point for this project was to map the key concepts of identity as it occurs in the three subjects of RE, Art and Citizenship, at Key Stage 3 in the English national curriculum.

Table 8.1 Mapping a shared concept across subjects

Art	Citizenship	Religious Education
1.3 Cultural understanding a) Engaging with a range of images and artefacts from different contexts, recognizing the varied characteristics of different cultures and using them to inform their creating and making. b) Understanding the role of the artist, craftsperson and designer in a range of cultures, times and contexts.	1.3 Identities and diversity: living together in the UK a) Appreciating that identities are complex, can change over time and are informed by different understandings of what it means to be a citizen in the UK. b) Exploring the diverse national, regional, ethnic and religious cultures, groups and communities in the UK and the connections between them. c) Considering the interconnections between the UK and the rest of Europe and the wider world. d) Exploring community cohesion and the different forces that bring about change in communities over time.	1.4 Identity, diversity and belonging a) Understanding how individuals develop a sense of identity and belonging through faith or belief. b) Exploring the variety, difference and relationships that exist within and between religions, values and beliefs.

Throughout this project students were given an A3 ring-bound book of cartridge paper to record their work rather than the usual school exercise book. The findings of this project showed an increase in self-awareness and acceptance of difference. The enquiries very often focused on difference and the ways in which we can make good judgements. Students who were underachieving began to make progress in their learning. Boys who were otherwise distracted and distractible became focused and ready to contribute their ideas into the shared investigation. The more able students were able to develop their thinking in ways which suited them: less constrained by the workings of regular classroom processes. Once the trust of all students was earned, the community began to move as one group. Perhaps the greatest lesson from this project was the value of engaging in philosophical enquiry with the same group every week. It can be difficult to find space for this in the secondary school and if we are serious about developing skills for the twenty-first century we need to reflect seriously upon it.

> 'I learned that I can help the world myself without having to have lots of money and equipment' (Becky)

> 'I changed through this project. I think more about other people, more about the environment and I feel more confident'. (Hannah)

> 'Artistic skills and enquiry are best … everyone enjoys these. If you learn with pleasure you remember, if you learn without pleasure you forget … ' (Saul)

> 'I learned to get along with people and not to be bossy or selfish. It has helped me in many ways'. (Bethany)

> 'I learned that I care about the world'. (Jonathan)

9

The philosophy club

If you are the first teacher to consider introducing the community of philosophical enquiry into your school then a helpful way to build up confidence in working in this new way can be to develop a 'philosophy club'. It may be that senior staff are looking for methods to introduce this approach into the life of the whole school or help develop thinking skills. In this situation too it will be helpful to consider the role that an extra-curricular 'philosophy club' could play in developing the community of philosophical enquiry in a school.

The person who is running the philosophy club has a great opportunity to work with an enthusiastic group of young people regularly and over a period of time. This is an excellent way to build experience and confidence in facilitating the enquiry process. Such a group could be brought together in a number of different ways.

Enrichment for gifted students

It is possible that the club could be established as an enrichment activity that could attract more able students in the school. If this were to be the starting-point it would be important to bring together a group of young people among whom there were already some existing friendships. This would ensure that the group would already have some cohesion between the members and it would provide an additional reason for them to meet each week while they are finding their feet with philosophy.

There is no doubt that gifted students benefit from this approach. They relish the opportunity to exchange their ideas with others and also to clarify their ideas in their own minds. They also find it a welcome opportunity to integrate their thinking, bringing together the material they are learning in science with the latest book they are reading or a programme on the radio or TV. This opportunity for interconnected thinking can hardly ever happen in a school where the curriculum is fragmented.

Such a philosophy club can be a safe haven for some gifted young people who may be very sensitive to the hustle and bustle of school life and who may relish the opportunity to engage in regular discussion of complex ideas with their peers.

A themed club with a philosophical approach

If the school would like to bring together a broader group of young people then another way to make progress with a philosophy club could be to open a 'global studies' club or use this as a way to commence a new school linking project. In these arenas it would be possible to develop particular concepts relating to the themes of the group. For example, with a 'global studies' or 'United Nations' club the principal themes to be explored would include justice, peace, education and human rights. Stimuli for the sessions could be selected to elicit questions about living in a globalized world. This kind of philosophical club would give many opportunities for linking with outside agencies and for students to be engaging philosophically with these issues.

The school council

It would be possible to envisage a school council running along the lines of a philosophical investigation. In this way the teacher/facilitator can be the one who supports the young people in raising and dealing with the key questions facing the school. It is to be hoped that, working philosophically with the questions, the young people would be able to develop strong arguments to support their requests and ideas. They would be able to discuss and explore possibilities with adults on a more equal footing as their thinking and reasoning skills are enhanced.

Resourcing the group

However the group begins, it will be important to allocate a small budget to support the purchase of some refreshments and opening materials. An excellent resource to support the start of work with the group is *The Philosophy Club*, a folder of excellent ideas written by Roger Sutcliffe and Steve Williams. Gradually, a collection of resources, picture-books and newspaper stories will be brought together. Over the time the facilitator of the club will become adept at spotting things that will be good stimuli to generate philosophical questions for an enquiry.

It may also be helpful to give the members of the group a folder or book in which to record their enquiries. The young people can keep copies of the stimuli for the enquiries in these books and make notes about the topics that have been discussed. Artistic students may like to draw or develop their ideas in alternative ways and the facilitator could provide the materials to support this.

Students who do not get the opportunity in other lessons to explore their ideas in creative and imaginative ways will welcome this club. It can be a haven for alternative thinkers who can sometimes find themselves isolated in the usual ways of working in regular classrooms. All in all, facilitating a philosophy club can be a great privilege for teachers as they get to know a small group of young people and watch them grow through the experience.

Opportunities for developing the community of philosophical enquiry in international education projects

10

In this chapter we consider two examples where the community of philosophical enquiry has been developed in different international projects. In both cases the work has facilitated understanding of complex issues across cultures. One project involved young people around the age of 13–16 years. The other was with students of about 17–22 years. In one project the key themes were citizenship and human rights and in the other peace, justice and sustainability. Having a clear focus on the philosophical themes in each context enabled the work to have a significant effect.

Given the capacity of the community of philosophical enquiry to support young people in their development of a sense of how they will live with others, this work could form a model for the development of intercultural understanding in education. These two examples of practice will show how the community of philosophical enquiry in this context can be a helpful environment for cultivating a moral imagination by offering young people the chance to think beyond their present experiences and to imagine new and different solutions to the concerns of the present age.

Facilitating the development of a school-linking project

The first international project we discuss is a school-linking project, developed over an extended period of almost a decade.

This school-linking project was initiated by the British Council in Mexico, bringing together an inner city 'Secundaria Tecnica' school in Mexico City and large comprehensive 11–18 school in the rural north-west of England. The UK government has for many years encouraged the development of school-linking projects between British schools and schools across the globe. This has been especially nurtured through the Department for International Development (DfID), a department established by the incoming Labour government following the general election of 1997. The British Council, as a branch of the Foreign Office, has bid for funding from DfID to support school-linking projects. In this case, the original vision was to bring 20 schools from Mexico City together with 20 schools in the UK.

From the beginning this link had a strong social aspect to the work. There was a long-term vision of developing young people's understanding of human rights and citizenship issues. Those involved from the UK side were interested in using the community of philosophical enquiry to support dialogue between students in the link, and this was agreed as a process for progressing with the link. The interschool relationship has developed through the work of philosophical enquiry. Almost at the start of the linking project we were able to meet Dr Tere de la Garza of the University of Ibero-America in Mexico City, a philosopher who has worked in depth with the community of philosophical enquiry. She helped us to form an academic and pedagogical framework. Teachers in both schools accessed training in the community of philosophical enquiry through their respective organizations in both countries.

Developing school-linking projects takes a great deal of time, energy and commitment from the teachers involved, and over the years there have been two ways in which the link has developed in both schools. The first of these has been embedding the link into the regular school curriculum so that young people from every class in the school can benefit from the interchange of cultures. An example of this in the UK school has been the development of a scheme of work for the Mexican Days of the Dead in religious education. An example of embedding the philosophical dimension of the link in the Mexican school has also been attempted through history, civics and ethics and geography.

The second way that the link has developed is through groups of young people having the opportunity to meet in exchange visits between the schools. During each of these visits the groups have engaged in several philosophical enquiries. The stimuli for the enquiries have been chosen to reflect the themes of the linking. For example on a visit to Mexico in 2007 we were able to develop a philosophical enquiry in the outdoors at the Popocatepetl National Park, exploring the work of environmental citizenship. A photograph of this can be seen in Plate 1. A second enquiry developed in the museum of anthropology, exploring the theme of identity (see Plate 2).

Those involved in the link on both sides of the Atlantic would say it was strengthened through involvement of the community of philosophical enquiry. This process has not only opened the students to new ways of thinking it has also facilitated the development of good friendships between the teachers in the link by ensuring that at the heart of conversations are those perennial human and philosophical issues by working with philosophical enquiry have become more able to discuss important questions.

We feel that this link has been successful for two key reasons. The first is that we agreed a pedagogical process for working together near the beginning. This meant that from the early stages of the link we were prepared to investigate problems and questions, resulting in the development of relationships that embody aspects of caring, critical, creative and collaborative thinking. The second reason is that the link had clear themes that lent themselves to philosophical analysis and conceptualization. These two things have meant that it was possible to develop philosophical exploration of the themes right from the beginning.

International Youth Congress, Chiapas, Mexico: peace, justice and sustainability

This was a conference for people aged 17–21, exploring some of the key issues facing our time through philosophical enquiry. This work is forming a philosophical pedagogy for education for sustainability.

The Congress has taken place each summer since July 2006, for two weeks in Chiapas, Mexico. It aims to offer a reflective, philosophical space, where those taking part can rehearse and investigate possible solutions to the key questions of our time with their peers. In so doing, skills and processes needed for considered decision-making and action can be developed and practised.

Children grow up primarily concerned about the immediate practical questions of their own lives – about their own immediate families, how to relate to siblings and parents, what to eat, or what to wear. When they move into the wider world there are other adults to please. If they are in school this will also include their teachers, employers and the variety of other adults who will also now guide their lives.

In early childhood, hopefully, there will be few great upheavals and few decisions to make. All this starts to change with the arrival of adolescence. Parents gradually slide into a second place – soon friends, peers and classmates become the most important points of reference. From 13 onwards adolescents will have to make some of the most important decisions in their lives. As adolescence continues, ideas that will influence their sense of empowerment to act in the wider world are formed. The

Students from UK, Mexico and Costa Rica forming philosophical questions in a small group as part of the Summer Youth Congress.

orientation towards the world developed at this stage of adolescence can have an impact that will influence the whole of the rest of their lives.

We can see the significance of this Congress in the light of increasing globalization. By meeting with other young people from different parts of the world in the community of philosophical enquiry existing conceptions can be reflected upon and revised in the light of shared experiences.

The Congress gives young people an opportunity to experience, on a daily basis, thoughtful reflection and action around the topics of social justice, sustainable development and peace education. At this point in their lives young people between 17 and 22 are starting to see themselves as part of a greater whole. There is an increasing awareness of what we all share and how we are all, in some way and to some extent, responsible for what happens.

Through the experiences of the Congress, participants are confronted with a variety of contexts where the issues that form the main guiding ideas are present. Some young people living comfortable 'Western' or 'occidental' lifestyles may never have to confront the realities of our present time. They may have a smooth pathway from school to higher education and into employment, never pausing to think about their contribution to the whole, never having the opportunity to be empowered to begin living a life where they are making a positive contribution to the future of our shared world.

This Congress aims to be a catalyst for making a difference. It builds on a vision to create a space where young people from different backgrounds can meet to explore key environmental, social, political and spiritual issues of our day, through the community of philosophical enquiry. The community of philosophical enquiry is a perfect context in which to explore the Congress themes. It offers a place where contemporary social, political and environmental philosophical concerns can be raised and allows for immense personal development. By working in community, exploring different ways of 'doing philosophy', by sharing ways of thinking and exploring new modes of reasoning, participants in the Congress are enabled to reflect deeply and rigorously about the experience of humankind. The international and intercultural experience of the summer Youth Congress, where the focus issues are pertinent to the survival of humanity, frames an opportunity for sharing with one's peers across the boundaries of continental perceptions, to formulate a considered position on these crucial matters. The Congress provides an opportunity to investigate an educational process of intercultural 'pluri-logue' or dialogue across many complex cultural boundaries. In so doing new paths to the future can be envisioned. Sharing philosophically reinforces awareness that we all are part of the same humanity, moved by a similar desire for peace, seeking a common fulfilment of our existence.

The Congress gathers most evenings, meeting in a circle to go through the important events of the day. Everyone is invited to develop philosophical questions pertinent to the experiences of the day with a small group of friends. A question is chosen for further exploration in the facilitated enquiry itself. Over the two weeks of the Congress these questions build upon each other; they develop, ebb and flow, allowing for an ever-deepening reflection on the themes of the Congress. The investigations are facilitated at least initially by the coordinators of the event who are both well experienced at working philosophically with young people in informal contexts.

The theoretical and philosophical roots of the community of philosophical enquiry are demonstrated in this work. It offers a framework where the ambiguity of truth can be exposed – where our experiences can be deconstructed, examined and then reformulated in light of the shared investigation. An aim of the Congress is that the encounter with philosophy that is on offer in the shared enquiries will support young people at a crucial point in their lives, nurturing courage and imagination to build a good future for all.

The small town of Chamula near to San Cristobal, Chiapas, is visited on the first day of the Congress. Here the people worship in the church, which was originally built as a Catholic church, but now offers a perfect example of syncretism in terms of religious practice, in a completely unique way. By observing the stark syncretism of cultures which is apparent in this place the participants have the opportunity to engage in a reflection, for example, about ideas of God, the role of faith and spirituality in people's lives and the multicultural nature of this society.

Tourists walk around the church, looking at the hundreds of candles lit on the floor, the figures of saints lined up against the wall in their wooden glass-panelled caskets, the drinking of 'posch' (the local liquor given to all involved in the ceremonies, including children) and the sacrifice of chickens by twisting and pulling their necks.

Later the community of the Congress spends time in an ecotourism centre in the Selva Lacandon. This offers an opportunity to experience the sounds, smells, flora and fauna of one of the last remnants of tropical rain forest left in Central America. Our descent in kayaks for two days in some of its rivers and our walks in the midst of abandoned archaeological sites, encountering all sorts of wildlife and with the explanations of our experienced guide, give all of the participants food for thought to develop the questions that would serve as a trigger for discussion every night of the Congress.

The ambiguities of Chiapas and the problems of globalization are clearly presented by experiencing and discussing the many political and social issues that are present in this area of the world. This makes the experience of the Congress more interesting but also more complex to understand. By reading before our visits we gained understanding of the social context and the reality of the places we visited and also ammunition to develop and defend arguments for or against different possible courses of action surrounding the issues involved.

The kinds of questions that have been raised by the work of the Congress would include:

What is a 'simple life' and how does it compare with a 'good life'?

Do animals have rights?

Does nature have rights?

Do we have any responsibility for taking care of our planet?

What is social justice?

Questions are also raised as a result of the international nature of the Congress, such as 'What does it mean to think globally and act locally?'

We are able to make if necessary more than one visit to Pro Natura, an organization that undertakes many different activities that have to do with the protection of the environment. The input of experts in various different fields – for example forestry, fair trade and organic coffee production – ensures that our enquiries are based upon research and are not solely an emotional response to the situations that we experience. The contact with Pro Natura allows us to know more about the neighbouring biosphere reserve and the many different activities and programmes that it has – for example, the certification of products as organic, or fair-trade issues. Students have the opportunity to investigate particular interests in detail. These and many other activities during the two weeks help us to think about the importance of unpacking the complexity of these issues and the things we could do about them.

Participants have a chance to interact with other young people of their own age, from indigenous communities who are living a very different style of life. Some of the young people we meet when visiting the communities were displaced from their communities because of political struggle during the 1990s, which became violent and divisive.

So we can see that this Congress has been designed to bring young people together who although from different contexts are all living through the same stage of life. Each of them has recently left school and they are all beginning to make major choices about what they will do with their lives: choices which will have a bearing on the next decades of their lives.

How can we make every voice heard in a global world?

Community of Philosophical Enquiry in the outdoors at the National Park, Popocatapetl near Mexico City.

The group forms into a community of philosophical enquiry, which grows in understanding throughout the period of the Congress. This provides a space for discussion and reflection about the ideas and questions the participants develop throughout the experience of the days of the Congress. In the last days of the Congress students are invited to choose a specific topic to develop in a more Comprehensive way and prepare a presentation to make to the rest of the group during the final night.

The long-term hope for the Congress, which is, as we have seen, rooted in the dialogical philosophical practice of the community of philosophical enquiry, is that those who participate are able, as a result, to formulate a more developed sense of the importance of the issues raised. It is our intention that through their philosophical reflections and investigations the young people will gain the motivation and courage to act upon these issues when they are present again in their lives. We hope that at least some of them will become agents for social change in the future in areas of sustainable development, peace education and/or social justice.

Two students' reflections on their experience of the Congress

Gerardo from Mexico City

When I read about the topic of the second Youth Congress I imagined how I could formulate a utopian, progressive plan for generating change in our society. I thought I would return with a clear plan to create consciousness about the problems we have created and their possible solutions through intercultural exchanges. But having gone through the experience of the Congress, I abandoned my original intentions and concentrated on some of my experiences with a different purpose. I introduced myself to the group as a stranger, but to my surprise I felt that I already knew them, when I really did not. I could see in their faces a thirst for going deeper into our experiences and developing a communitarian spirit.

There is much complaint about individualism, in response to the questionable progress that rules our lives in the cities. In my case I came to this Congress to enrich my own point of view. I hoped to break certain stereotypes and to awaken the mysticism I have always felt for Chiapas and I hoped to share in its natural beauty and spaces.

However, the experience turned out to have a different consequence from the one I anticipated. To explain this I find it helpful to consider the concept of 'Chaos'.

According to Pierre-Simon Laplace, if we could know the speed and position of all particles in the universe at one point in time, then we could predict the past and the future. However, Henri Poincaré said that chance is only a measure of man's ignorance. He pointed out that there is no free will. And with regard to this I want to comment on an experience during the Congress. When we were in San Juan Chamula and at the home of Angelitas, a woman living in Lacanjá, there were certain things that happened that made me think a great deal. I became aware that superstition and faith are a key in terms of locating the origin of the happiness and prosperity of people in these regions. If we understand these behaviours as a sign of ignorance, according to a scientific point of view, then I think this ignorance is not bad. I just think people accommodate their circumstances to what is best for them.

For example, if I brainwashed an indigenous person from Chamula with my way of thinking, I would create disequilibrium in his ways of thinking, which may be disadvantageous for his own survival. With this I want to say that we all create our own truths for our own survival.

These are given to us through our own experience and we just need to accept them and be patient with them. We came to realize that it is a mistake to romanticize too much about the way indigenous people live and think in Chiapas. At the beginning of days together we thought that living in community would be the best solution to all our problems. But I think that it simply won't work. It would be like trying to walk on water or swim inland. With this I mean to say that these communities live as they do because they need it for survival.

In conclusion I think the key to happiness is accepting the world we have, questioning morality without denying it in order to understand nature and everything that happens. Not labelling it as black or white, but green. My thinking is an ongoing process.

Hannah from Cumbria in the UK

Hannah wrote about her experience of being sick while in the forest and of the realizations that she came to. She describes how while alone

and feeling very sick, it was just me. I could feel the heat and hear the sounds of the rainforest. I remembered how when walking through the jungle we asked our guide what the extremely loud buzzing and the high-pitched piercing noises were. I expected him to say that it was a rather large exotic animal. However, he informed us that in fact it was a very small insect – a cicada.

These insects, although so small, have a large impact on the sound of the rainforest. This made me think about the impact one person could have as a small individual in comparison with the scale of this vast universe. Although we may not realize that we are having any effect at all, because our actions seem so small and insignificant, in fact we do! When small individual actions form together, larger actions that have positive and negative effects can begin.

Unfortunately many actions by many individuals and groups of people are having devastating effects on our world. The food we eat, the cars we drive, all add greenhouse gases into the atmosphere. From reflecting on these facts we can get an idea of exactly how much impact we are having as individuals. Linked with this and feeling ill lying in the forest, I began to think about the impact humans are having on the planet.

When in an enquiry based on the subjects of the good life and the simple life, I defined the good life as a life you choose, a virtuous life and a joy in life, whilst also helping others to have this. I think we have a definite moral obligation to consider others when we make decisions about our actions. When we affect people's lifestyles and happiness in a negative way, we are obviously not caring for the joy in their life. If we are harming others in the world then we are not really living a good life. This is the negative impact humans can have; however, this works equally with the positive!

In a wider sense, countries have the ability to help other countries in terms of money lending and support and can therefore make positive impacts. So, as we are currently having a very negative impact on our world, we must look at the positive actions we can participate in to make a good impact and stop the changes from being irreversible.

If we encourage others to think and act in ways to improve the negative effects we're having in everyday life, they may tell other people who may act, and who may tell others who'll do the same. Essentially a whole stream of links begin to occur which can make a huge difference. This difference may be large and may have come from a small simple action of telling someone something; it may have been insignificant to the person starting the chain, a simple conversation they thought nothing more about, but in fact a large impact has been made.

This leads me to conclude that we should never underestimate the small actions we do in our lives; they can have large positive and negative consequences. We may think that we cannot make a difference, but we have the power to make changes, big and small.

Just like the tiny insects have huge impacts on the sounds of the jungle, we as small humans can have massive impacts on our world. In relation to the question I came to, which has led me to these thoughts, there can be two directions. To look at the negative impact we can have as humans, but also the positive. How much impact can one person have in relation to the topics of this Congress? We can have a lot more impact than we can perceive and we shouldn't underestimate this.

I now have a lot more faith in my ability to bring about change and affect the lives of others, as a young insignificant girl, from a small town in England, who maybe isn't so insignificant.

- How many different contexts can you think of where you have the opportunity to have philosophical conversations with the young people with whom you come into contact?
- How have you supported the young people with whom you meet to reflect on their place in the world as future adults?

11 Implications for training facilitators

The surest way to guarantee the best outcomes in the classroom with philosophy for children anywhere in the world is to ensure that the facilitator who will work with the young people in this new way is suitably prepared. Most aspects of regular teacher-training in British universities at this time do not in any way prepare new teachers to work with young people in this more informal way. This is quite likely to be the case if the student is undertaking a three- or four-year bachelors degree in education and almost certain to be the case if the training is a one-year postgraduate certificate in education (PGCE).

Philosophy for children is not a conventional educational approach that requires the teacher to follow an outline plan or a programme published in an established manual or government curriculum document. Working effectively with the community of philosophical enquiry is a much more complex project than we might at first think.

Essential areas for consideration in teacher education in the community of philosophical enquiry

Five important areas of development are needed when someone is preparing to work with the community of philosophical enquiry in the classroom and particularly with young people at this important and transformatory stage of their lives:

- A good understanding of the background and development of the work of the community of philosophical enquiry since the 1960s. This will give teachers a clearer idea of what it is they hope to gain by working with their students in this way. We can call these 'theoretical skills'.

- A growing understanding of philosophical concepts and the history of philosophical ideas. A good working understanding of philosophy is essential if teachers are to be able to recognize and develop the philosophical thinking in young people. These are essential in order to be able to push the enquiry to be a truly philosophical investigation and not just a friendly 'chat'. We can call these 'philosophical skills'.

- Particularly for those going to work with adolescents, a grasp is needed of what psychologists and sociologists are saying about the present situation of young people who are growing through a certain stage of life. We can call these 'adolescent developmental tasks' or 'psychological development skills'. It is very important to note that the community of philosophical enquiry is not a stage theory of pedagogy. Rather, those who work with philosophical enquiry prefer to focus on how the community of philosophical enquiry can support the development of children or young people at any particular stage of their life. So it is the other way round.

- More open pedagogical facilitation skills. Those working more informally with young people – such as social workers or youth workers – may have a good start with these skills. We can call them 'pedagogical skills'.

- A good working knowledge of the development of thinking skills – in particular a very good understanding of reasoning and what makes a good argument. There is some crossover here between the psychological skills and philosophical skills. But we may broadly call these 'thinking and reasoning skills'.

Clearly the community of philosophical enquiry is not a process where teachers can research and rehearse a formula in the same way that Ofsted criteria can be coached and rehearsed. Producing facilitators who can nurture moral imagination in the young people with whom they are working, will not be a simple matter of developing certain teacher 'characteristics' or 'competencies' in order to reach a certain 'approved' manner of being. On the contrary, teachers confident with working in the community of enquiry must be prepared to make mistakes, to take risks and to be creative and imaginative. This work requires them to become prepared to respond repeatedly to the original and unexpected contributions of young people. In this way the teacher/facilitator will be in the best position to develop the moral imagination of the young people with whom he or she is working. It is through this creativity that new solutions to difficult situations can be explored and new possibilities sought. This can be immensely liberating for young people who will ultimately be responsible for working towards a good future for all. The alternative, as we have discussed earlier, is that young people are disempowered by the world situation and lose interest or, even worse, become disaffected.

To be able to do this effectively requires that teachers not only think of predetermined 'learning objectives' but that they are able to respond spontaneously to the contributions of and the lead taken by the young people, allowing the community of philosophical enquiry to give birth to new understandings and possibilities. This is much more like being part of a jazz ensemble than the conductor of a classical orchestra. It requires teachers to change their attitude and perception of the potential of the young people in front of them – to see the young people as valuable human beings with visions and dreams of their own. This is a true personalizing of learning and a profound understanding of the depths of an educational vision for the well-being of all for the twenty-first century. This work requires those involved in facilitating philosophical enquiries to form their own objectives for education as part of a vision of a hoped-for society.

The teacher or other professional who intends to work with philosophy for children will need a certain understanding of philosophy, psychology and pedagogy. We hope it is clear how these areas will work together.

In this section we draw on the experience of the Mexican Federation for Philosophy for Children and work that has developed in the UK.

Training in the community of philosophical enquiry in the UK has been developed through the Society for the Advancement in Philosophical Enquiry and Reflection in Education (SAPERE). It is delivered by well-prepared trainers who are based around the country. The UK training is in three phases. Level 1 takes 10 hours and is followed by level 2, which requires 24 hours. Moving from level 1 to level 2 depends on completion of 12 communities of enquiry. Level 2 is followed by level 3, which requires a further 24 hours training. An assignment reflecting in detail upon part of an enquiry is a necessary requirement. There is also an assignment following level 3. These three together form something similar to the first module of the Mexican Federation diploma in philosophy for children. For more information on SAPERE training see the contact details toward the end of the book.

How much philosophy is needed to facilitate for philosophical enquiry?

First let us look at the need for the teacher/facilitator to have a good grasp of philosophical ideas. A question that immediately arises is how much philosophy teachers must know to be able to develop the community of philosophical enquiry with their students. Some would say very little or none; others would prefer that teacher/facilitators are graduates in philosophy, or at least that they have part of their degree in philosophy.

Our answer is that it is certainly desirable that the teacher should know something about philosophy in order to be able to begin to work with children and young people. It is perhaps more important that they have the motivation to know more about philosophy so that their knowledge and understanding increases gradually and so that there is a constant awareness of the importance of philosophy in their work with the students. What then do we mean when we say the teacher should know something about philosophy?

In Mexico, teachers taking an introductory course in philosophy for children study for approximately 35 hours. This entitles them to be able to have access to novels and manuals that were written by Lipman and translated into the Mexican context by Eugenio Echeverria, appropriate to the level in which they are working with children and young people. During these 35 hours training in philosophy for children the teachers are given a supportive input of philosophy, which allows them to get started. This will include something about epistemology (theory of knowledge) and logic and reasoning, together with an introduction to ethics.

Fortunately, in Mexico and other Latin American countries philosophy is part of the curricula for the baccalaureate or end of high school examination at 18 years of age. The majority of high schools in Mexico require that all students take courses in the history of the philosophical thought; some also require ethics and logic.

However, unfortunately, the way in which the majority of the philosophy courses are taught in the high school serves rather to turn teachers and their students against philosophy, instead of transmitting a sense of wonder at the possibility of philosophy and an interest in exploring beyond the philosophy that they have worked on in school.

The truth is that the majority of teachers who want to introduce philosophy for children in their practice know very little or nothing of philosophy before taking the introductory course. In the UK there is a similar situation: very few teachers have studied any philosophy at all and may have even picked up a slightly negative impression about philosophy. Many certainly have the idea that it is perhaps something only for very clever people or people who cannot handle reality in some way.

However, the very least we must hope for through training in philosophy for children is that teachers are able to explain and demonstrate for example to a parent or carer of a young person they are working with, or perhaps another teacher (or even to a philosopher) is the way in which the work of the community of philosophical enquiry *really is* philosophy. For example, we need to show what it is that the young people are doing through the dialogue in the community that is philosophical. If someone came into an enquiry, how would they recognize that it was philosophy and not something else like a therapeutic situation? Most importantly, could the teacher concerned explain this clearly?

In order to enable teachers to do this they will need to have some understanding of the main concepts involved in the different branches of philosophy – for example, aesthetics, ethics, epistemology, metaphysics and logic. They will need to have an idea of around five or ten key concepts or key questions or problems that have been studied in each of these areas of philosophy throughout history. In this way they will be able to recognize when these key concepts, questions or problems arise in their communities of enquiry. Of course, the children and adolescents are perfectly able to have a discussion about any of these topics without knowing about the history of philosophy. But it is important that the teacher knows enough to give the students a chance to appreciate that to be concerned with these perennial problems is a matter of wider human concern.

When working with teachers in these areas we are supporting a process that enables teachers to develop a philosophical dimension in their own lives and a philosophical understanding of their life experiences. We consider this to be one of the most important objectives of the work of the community of philosophical enquiry. What we want for the young people in our care has to be something we are also working on as teachers in our own personal and professional lives. In this respect the community of philosophical enquiry is quite distinctive. It is not just something that teachers do to students in order for them to perform better in examinations. In working with the process ourselves we are transformed both in our professional work and our personal lives. We have to become more openminded and more open to different possibilities in order to facilitate this in the enquiry. For this reason people have been known to describe the work with philosophical enquiry as more like a way of life than a pedagogical strategy. Of course this was what Socrates said when he suggested that an unreflected life was not worth living. As teachers working with this process we are compelled to reflect upon the relationship with our work and our whole lives. This can be what makes our educational practice most worthwhile.

In addition to these aspects, it is important that the teacher has practised the identification and formulation of philosophical questions and that they know how to transform a non-philosophical question into one that is philosophical. In this way the teacher can have some idea how to prevent the community of enquiry being slowed down with non-philosophical considerations. Initial training will, by its nature, be limited for time, so it will also be necessary for the educator planning to work with young people philosophically to have a grasp, for example, of when it will be useful to develop criteria regarding a concept in order to clarify its meaning in a philosophical question. It is then necessary to understand what criteria *are* and also how to work with them in the enquiry. This can be illustrated by considering the concept of 'friend'. In an enquiry with a question oriented around the concept 'friend', such as 'Can someone you have not met be your friend?' it may be helpful at some point to think carefully about what the word 'friend' means. A student may suggest looking into a dictionary for a definition. Generally in a philosophical enquiry this will not be helpful because a definition is just one view of the word. What can be more helpful philosophically is to reflect in the community on what would count as a 'friend'. This list of things that we could say would count as a 'friend' would be said to be 'criteria' of the concept 'friend'. As we have discussed earlier, clarifying concepts in a philosophical question will be an important stage in working with a philosophical question in a community of philosophical enquiry. For a question to be interesting philosophically it needs to offer the opportunity of reflection on concepts in relation to other ideas, for instance in the example above in relation to the ideas of 'someone you have not met'.

In general there are three guiding principles for defining a philosophical question:

- A philosophical question is controversial: people will not agree exactly upon how to respond to it , and it is therefore open to discussion.

- It does not have an easy answer and promotes disagreement in order to move forward in understanding the question.

- The philosophical question will be one that has importance in some way for all humanity.

An example of how to develop a capacity in working with philosophical questions can be for small groups of teachers or students to form philosophical questions and then to identify the branches of philosophy that are addressed in the questions. Examples might include:

- How can we know if something is true? (**epistemology**)

- When can we consider that something is just? (**ethics**)

- Can we ever be really free? (**political philosophy**)

- When we can say that something is beautiful? (**aesthetics**)

- How do we know if something is good or bad? (**ethics**)

In conclusion, probably the most important thing for an introductory training in the community of philosophical enquiry in terms of philosophy is for there to be a good understanding of the nature of philosophy and its different branches, and further for there to be motivation to go and seek out more philosophy!

What aspects of psychology will be necessary to facilitate the community of philosophical enquiry?

In considering how much knowledge of adolescent psychological development should be understood by teachers who are preparing to work with adolescents in the community of philosophical enquiry we need to think how this will help in facilitating philosophical ideas that aim to nurture moral awareness and imagination. In most cases, regular teacher-training programmes in the UK include little about the psychological and emotional changes during adolescence. However, social work and other professional training for work with adolescents, such as youth work, will have had input on these topics. Teachers may have heard of Piagetian stage theory but probably little else. They may have a grasp of the cognitive changes of understanding and physical development through adolescence but it is unlikely that a teacher in the UK has thought much about the important qualitative or emotional changes that will influence the ways in which adolescents think. It is even less likely that teachers in the UK have received any training in identity development unless they have been able to take a psychology degree. During training to prepare someone to work with adolescents in the community of philosophical enquiry it will therefore be important to introduce some theoretical background relating to the concerns about adolescent identity development, as discussed in Chapter 2.

In addition to practical input on adolescent psychological, emotional and identity development, in order to develop a high level of understanding of the potential for the work of enquiry with adolescents it may be helpful to have an understanding of the work of other thinkers such as Vygotsky. In particular, Vygotsky's work on the 'zone of proximal (or potential) development' has a particular relevance here.

It will be important to illustrate how this relates to the work of the young person in the dialogue taking place in the community of philosophical enquiry. Vygotsky's work can help us understand, for example, the reasons why young people may be able to change their minds by hearing other people's thoughts on a question. Vygotsky suggests strongly that young people will benefit from learning with and from their peers, particularly those who know more about an issue. For him, learning and growing into competent adults is a social matter. The social interaction in terms of collaborative thinking that takes place between the students in the community of philosophical enquiry can most certainly promote and support psychological growth in each of them, as discussed in Chapter 2. For the facilitator of the enquiry to understand these processes will certainly be most advantageous.

In addition, for teachers and other professionals who have received little educational theory in their training it will also be helpful to refer to the work of thinkers such as Bruner and Ausubel. It is important to note why the work of these writers has had more influence on the development of theory internationally in the community of philosophical enquiry than that of, for example, Piaget . This is because Piaget has emphasized a staged theory of development. Matthew Lipman, when developing the community of philosophical enquiry, was clear that this is not perceived as a reality through the work of the community of philosophical enquiry. The experience of those working in philosophical enquiry over the past 40 years is that experience and learning precedes development rather than the other way round – contrary to what is suggested by stage theories such as those of Piaget and Kohlberg. This view leads us to suggest that if we work with young people in more subtle ways, supporting their learning and understanding, their development and emotional and psychological well-being will be advanced through the promotion of discussions with their peers in a collaborative social context. During the discussions young people will have the opportunity to, for example, question their presuppositions, learn to make good inferences, identify contradictions, and grow in the capacity to correct their own ways of thinking (or change their minds), based on the things they discover in the enquiry. They learn to build on the ideas of the others and to work together with these skills in a real context with their peers. . This is more relevant to real life and the development of the moral imagination than formalized 'thinking-skills' exercises.

In the training of educators it is essential that there is also sufficient time for practice in facilitating enquiries both with young people in their classes and also with other teachers. One of the main challenges facing those new to working with this process is how to gain enough practical experience in the work of the community of philosophical enquiry. This is important because the community of philosophical enquiry is not a theoretical model but one that is best learned through practical experience. It is preferable that those preparing to work with the community of philosophical enquiry can discover for themselves the things we have been discussing in this chapter and gain the tools to be able to advance the work of the philosophical dialogue and enquiry with their students. We cannot gain this just by reading alone.

Those preparing to work with the community of philosophical enquiry need to live the experience of the community dialogue for themselves and ideally feel for themselves how their thinking develops as a result of being questioned by their companions. They need to experience for themselves how previously fixed ways of thinking can move and change through listening to the voice of others in a community of dialogue. It can be most helpful for them to experience the open space of the community of philosophical enquiry so that they are able to return to their own situations to transform and enrich their own practice in their familiar environment. Most importantly, it is very helpful to experience how thinking and dialoguing in critical and caring ways can support their own development in the light of the contributions and collaboration of others.

What aspects of pedagogical understanding will be necessary to facilitate the community of philosophical enquiry?

In the UK the concept of pedagogy is not well known. However, elsewhere in Europe and Latin America developing what is termed 'pedagogical understanding' is considered an important element of preparing to work with young people and children. We can best begin by expanding what this area of learning is.

Pedagogy can be defined as the 'art or science of being a teacher'. In the context of the community of philosophical enquiry this not only refers to teachers but to all those who are preparing to become facilitators. Pedagogy is something that helps us to understand how young people learn and in what ways the adults who are with them can help or hinder the process. For those working in the area of philosophical and dialogical enquiry, there are many factors to take into account.

When beginning to work in the community of enquiry the facilitator will bring numerous presuppositions about education, about the way young people are in the world, about their needs. Over the years there has been a great deal written about philosophical enquiry, building from the work of Matthew Lipman. This is a philo-sophical approach to pedagogy that takes into account the psychological needs of young people. However, it is not a prescriptive view about education in the way that other well-known pedagogies are, such as the Montessori system or that devised by Froebel. For us, working with philosophical enquiry with the view to nurturing the moral imagination, the aim is to become more knowledgeable and reflective about theories primarily in the area of philosophy, but also of psychology, social theory and so on.

There have been many influences on the development of this aspect of the work over the years. Initially the formative thinker in the field was John Dewey and in particular his work on democracy and education, but others coming from critical theory, such as Paulo Freire, were also influential. What is clear though is that a training scheme for teachers in the community of philosophical enquiry should offer a wide range of reading. It is important that this is considered in a reflective way and also in the spirit of enquiry. It should include some major texts that have been written by those investigating the value of this approach over the years. A detailed reading list is offered at the end of this book, which includes information about the Lipman novels and manuals themselves.

Nurturing a moral imagination

The way that the facilitator relates to the students will give them much to reflect upon and could facilitate a transformation towards better coexistence between the members of the community. This, in turn, may lead the young people to reflect upon how relationships between people should or could be in a social democracy and further envision new possibilities for the global challenges ahead.

Throughout the philosophical enquiry in a dialogical community students are given many opportunities to reflect upon the different subjects and topics presented to them. An important aspect of philosophical enquiry is the way it can be applied to any subject. It is a *process* or a manner of working. This reflection helps the young people in their ability to build a thoughtful response to two of the most important questions we can ever ask in our lives: 'What kind of a person do I want to become?' and 'What kind of a world do I want to live in and leave to future generations?' The work of the community of philosophical enquiry supports young people in their personal projects but it also engages them in a wider social project. Furthermore, the community of philosophical enquiry helps them to develop the means by which they can link the two together to form a consistent way of thinking and living. This is conducive to psychological well-being.

If students are to be able to do this, it will be imperative for the teacher/facilitator to be engaged with this kind of reflection as well. The facilitator of the dialogue community must emphasize the importance of congruence between thinking, saying and doing. The teacher becomes a model for consistency between thought, word and action.

For these reasons it is helpful if facilitators continue to develop their understanding of the process of philosophical enquiry and to enable this, some schools have organized philosophical enquiries as part of the whole-school teacher professional development. We find that in addition to the teacher developing her facilitation skills, over time, understanding of the potential for the community of philosophical enquiry grows as well. As the teacher/facilitator's understanding grows, so she can facilitate the work of the students more carefully. For this reason, more or less half of the training time is actual engagement in philosophical enquiry.

In summary, when thinking about the training requirements to enable someone to work successfully with the community of philosophical enquiry, it is helpful to be reminded of its main objectives. There are three main aims:

- To open up a space where young people can practise and develop a variety of ways of thinking and reasoning.
- To support young people in their exploration of philosophical concepts and to help them discover a philosophical dimension in their lives.
- To explore ethical questions and by so doing form a series of moral guidelines for young people that give direction to their actions in their daily lives.

The facilitator's task is to facilitate the dialogue so that adolescents learn to listen to others, to build on their ideas, to give examples and counter-examples in support of their points of view, so that they analyse alternatives, predict consequences and so forth. In these ways young people practise and develop their reasoning at the same time as they become involved in the enquiries. Here there is space to explore, to deconstruct and reconstruct their own experience with the support of a social engagement with their peers.

As facilitators progress in their understanding of the process of philosophical enquiry they come to realize the immensity and significance of the task to be carried out in the classroom. Any training of teachers to become facilitators has to open minds to this kind of realization and support a changing vision of the role of an educator in educational institutions of the twenty-first century. The new facilitator needs to appreciate how different this is from the usual way of working with young people where there is a more formal focus on teaching and learning and the aquisition of predetermined knowledge.

12

Student voices: three case-studies

To close this book we include three pieces of writing from young people who have had much experience of communities of philosophical enquiry during secondary school. We asked them to write their own reflections on the way this process has supported the development of their thinking.

The first contribution is written by Vicky Stringer who was involved in a philosophy club in her secondary school for five years as well as exploring with this process in her regular classroom. She was part of the Mexican linking project and attended the summer Congress in Chiapas. At the time of writing this piece she is studying philosophy at Edinburgh University. Jeremy Dykes, who writes next, is a physics student at Durham who was a member of the same philosophy club as Vicky. The third piece is by Mark Borthwick, who at the time of writing is in the first year of GCSE. He expresses in his own words how he sees a gap in current secondary education.

Vicky Stringer: reflections from the Second International Youth Congress, Chiapas, August 2007

Introduction

'Education' is a word that encompasses not only teaching and learning specific skills but also the more profound idea of communicating knowledge, the cultivation of positive judgement and the development of wisdom. Another fundamental aspect of education is the imparting of *culture* from generation to generation. In the light of this, I support Freire's view that education can either be used to maintain the status quo or it can contribute to the process of liberation. Whatever education is, I am certain that it cannot be neutral.

I write now on this subject as a result of our visit to a school in Yapteclum, a small town in the highlands of Chiapas about two hours drive north of San Cristobal de las Casas. While we were there we learnt something of the people's lives and education and soon realized we had completely different attitudes not only towards the societies in which we live but within these societies themselves. Rafea, the man who had helped in setting up the school, drew this to our attention in our different responses to the question 'What do you hope to do after your current education?' Whilst we said that we were going to do a particular subject because we either enjoyed it or were good at it, the Mexican young people attending the part-time school in Yapteclum said that they would use their education to help their community. This stark difference in our attitudes to our own communities and to the point of education was highlighted by Rafea, who told us that he believed that there were three different types or groups of people in the world: individualistic, personalistic or community-minded. Rafea believed that we came under the personalistic group of people as, although we had not chosen our futures based on the promise of money, we had chosen to do things for our own personal pleasure, not to help our community. This was clearly different from the assumptions of the young people from Yapteclum, who were obviously more community-orientated.

I began to think what had made this difference in attitude towards our communities or societies, and also about which of the three groups demonstrated the best way to live. However, when thinking about these questions, instead of getting answers, a whole host of other questions and musings came. The one continuous thread running through all these thoughts was the concept of education and how it has shaped and is shaping the ways of life in each of our two countries.

Education and society run along in parallel with each other, especially in Britain, where school is compulsory from the age of 5 to 16. Education creates society, and in turn, society creates education. In this way, education in Britain is used to maintain the status quo. However, does this policy work in a world that is always changing?

Education, as I experience it growing up in the north of England, had been mainly focused on academic subjects – in other words, subjects that can secure you the best and most well-paid career. This is reflected in the makeup of the British economy, where the majority of people work in the 'services sector', encompassing jobs such as teaching and nursing. Therefore great emphasis is placed on subjects such as maths and the sciences as these are the areas in which the most well-paid careers can be followed and this, in turn, will also maintain the image of our developed and until now, highly economically stable country.

In Mexico, in indigenous communities, it is possible that education in schooling terms is different from that in England because our societies or communities are different. After all, education does not only refer to the scholarly process in general but also the process of learning skills and ways of understanding the world, which includes learning from other people. This may be more likely to happen in a close-knit community. When this type of learning takes place this brings the community together and this in turn drives the desire for a close community in the next generation.

However, this does not tell us why they work in such a close or community-minded way. A question that came up in our enquiry one night was: 'Do they work as a community in this way because they need to?' I think I would tend to agree with this statement as, in an unstable environment, it is better to work together as a team because you all have a common interest – the survival of not only yourself, but your community as this encompasses not only your friends and family but the land on which you depend. For example, for the individual to survive it is necessary for the survival of the community. Similarly, in England, for our community to remain constant in the way it functions now, it is necessary that we think in an individualistic way as we place high prestige on the idea or concept of the entrepreneur.

Another aspect that it is important to consider when regarding these differences is the concept of land. Here in Mexico the land is very important, for, as Rafea said to us: 'The community must support the land, and in return the land will support the community.' This is also quite an alien concept to us in England as we have already destroyed our land and therefore we do not need to work together to protect it.

Yet another issue that arose in our discussion in Yapteclum was the concept of identity. One question asked of the people there was: 'Do you feel a connection with the ancient Mayans?' It turned out that many of them felt a strong affinity with their ancestors and believed that if more of their philosophies or beliefs existed today, then perhaps the world today would be a better place, as they believed that the Mayans had more respect for nature and their natural resources. The people also seemed to have a strong sense of identity, of themselves and with each other, and I wondered if this sense of identity meant that they worked more as a community, to protect their land but also their ancestry. This struck me especially when Rafea said: 'You can burn my branches and my trunk, but you can never burn my roots.' This strong sense of identification with the past is missing in England and I wondered if this lack of common or strong ancestry means that we don't identify with each other as much in England, and therefore find it more difficult to work as a community. In England we do not appear to have a strong shared past to identify ourselves with, but I believe we still have a strong sense of self, and this may be encouraged rather than stifled by our individualistic society.

What kind of education can be used to bridge this gap in our societies? And which, if any, of these approaches, individualistic or community, is better?

I think a philosophical approach to education offers a simple answer to this question as it encompasses both the individualistic and community-minded perspectives. This is because different points of view are not only welcomed but encouraged in philosophical discussion. This is the individualistic approach, offering entirely personal viewpoints to the community in order to build up an answer to the question. An individualistic viewpoint also understands that it is perfectly acceptable to disagree with someone as this enables the different opinions that can allow your own thoughts and opinions to grow, permitting not only intellectual growth but also spiritual growth. However, from a community or communitarian perspective we come to understand that, despite these disagreements, we can still listen to one another and even if you still disagree with each other at the end of the discussion you can still try and get a better understanding of the other person's viewpoint, and this also enables you to grow more as a person, including emotionally, and helps you develop the skill of empathy rather than sympathy, which can sometimes bring misinterpretations.

However, before the two communities could work together with philosophy there would have to be some convergence of the two different approaches or attitudes. Firstly, individualists would have to learn to listen to other points of view and accept that their viewpoint is not the only viewpoint, and also learn how to work together as a community – hence the term 'community of enquiry'. This would involve being able to build upon other people's points of view and work together as a team in trying to solve the question posed by that community. Similarly, communitarians would also have to change, perhaps even more so than individualists, as they would have to learn that having a different point of view was acceptable and they would have to learn to ask more questions and think in a more critical or cynical way. This would be especially difficult if they had been conditioned by the community to adopt the viewpoints of that community. In that situation it would be very difficult for them to be able to think freely for themselves. However, the concept of working together to solve a problem or difficult question would come naturally to communitarians, as they would use this method within their community on a regular basis.

So it seems that, with a little convergence on both sides, philosophy is the happy medium that sits between the two extremes of the individualist and the communitarian. You cannot have a successful enquiry with people who are at either one of these two extremes. However, does that mean you have to be in the second category that Rafea mentioned – the personalistic? To me, it depends on this category's definition. If personalistic means a mix of the traits found in both the individualistic and the communitarian characteristics then I would tend to agree with this category. However, personally I also disagree with categories, as to me they sound too fixed, as if they cannot be changed, and I think that this is a very wrong assumption.

The use of philosophy to bridge the gap between individuals and communities is also supported by John Dewey, who believed that the formation of the mind was a communal process. Not only that, but he believed that the individual is only a meaningful concept when regarded as an inextricable part of his or her society, and similarly the society has no meaning apart from its realization in the lives of its individuals.

Earlier on I asked whether the individualistic approach or the communitarian approach is better. Hopefully, you will realize that this question is irrelevant and that the real question is how to bridge the gap between the different viewpoints to encompass the positive attributes of the two different approaches. For me, philosophy is the answer. As Paulo Freire has reflected in different places in his writing, education is something in society that can be used in the maintenance of the status quo or it can contribute to the process of liberation. In this way I believe that philosophy is liberation and because of this I also believe that philosophy should be an integral part of everyone's education, not only in Britain and Mexico, but in the rest of the world as well.

This was how it has worked for me. I came across philosophical enquiry when I was 12 and it was a revelation to me. Finally there was a chance to explore my questions, thoughts and beliefs with other people like me and share experiences in order to work towards finding answers to some of the most complex questions. In this way over the years I found myself challenging my own beliefs and preconceptions even more, and speaking to other people helped me think about ideas that I had never thought of before. As I have heard other people's experiences and ideas, these have in turn shaped my own and allowed me to consider questions from many different points of view, and I have found this a very important part of the person that I am today.

Jeremy Dykes, physics student, Durham University, UK

I started the 'philosophy for children' style of thinking when I was 12. Since then it has had a marked effect in my learning both at school and onwards to university. The community of philosophical enquiry opened up new ways of thinking about a problem – be it in physics, the field that I now study, or in a general discussion with employers, peers and friends. I also had the opportunity to develop some facilitation skills myself and facilitated some philosophical enquiries in maths with students in the lower part of the school.

One of the major advantages of conducting philosophical enquiries with students is that it creates a space for giving young people the chance to practise making their own questions and forming their own opinions based on a discussion of a stimulus. Then, when this opinion is questioned, a stable enquiry enables the logical train of thought to be examined. In terms of learning the skill of critical examination it is crucial, but also in a society where peer pressure is strong the willingness to stand firm on a solid argument is very important.

Albert Einstein said: 'You do not really understand something unless you can explain it to your grandmother.' From practice gained in understanding another's train of thought I really have explained some quantum mechanics to my grandmother – whether she entirely understood or not is a different question! That aside, it is the ability to produce metaphors and give other examples and counter-examples that are understandable to the audience, be it an audience of students, colleagues or grand-parents, that enables the best and most accurate communication of thoughts and ideas.

As I have moved into the role of facilitating my own enquiries, new insights into the effect of P4C on students have been gained. I now apply my philosophical skills as a consultant for Cambridge University on the Motivate Maths project. This pro-ject aims to enable students to gain an insight into mathematics through innovative methods. In the day-long conferences we examine a variety of stimuli and the stu-dents are asked to discuss, in a logical manner, what they think or have learnt. The progress in one day is astounding and the students comment that the logical skills learnt remain with them – surely of crucial importance to their education.

Yet the skill of undertaking logical argument is not the only one they gain. A fruitful discussion revolves around respect for another's opinion and trying to 'get into the other person's shoes'. All philosophers must learn that opinions should not be immediately discounted but that each should be assessed and considered.

The philosophy work at Ulverston Victoria High School has enabled students to participate in SAPERE conferences, has links around the world, and shows that it is not just adult facilitators with many qualifications who can lead successful enquiries, but that students, with the experience gained from many discussions, are just as able to host complex enquiries. My work for Cambridge University has demonstrated that learning philosophy is not always a long process, that much progress can be made in a day and that this progress has lasting effects upon the students who take part in discussions.

We have seen here that philosophical enquiry has effects, for participants and facilitators, on many levels. These include respect for opinions and points of view, creating and presenting logical trains of thought and communicating complex ideas to a range of audiences. These are invaluable skills for all members of a society that is facing many changes and uncertainties in the future.

Mark Borthwick, age 15

One of the biggest problems with the schooling system today is coping with the (potentially) ethically barren curriculum. The National Curriculum is tapered to build 'successful' young people, but ideas of what that 'being successful' is are wide and varied. Is a community of enquiry a forum within which a more ethical side of a subject can be explored? Can this be an effective engine for students to explore information with such things in mind?

From our nation's point of view, a successful person is possibly a wealthy, punctual taxpayer. From a cynical point of view, it would be great for the leaders of our nations if we never looked over the parapet and never questioned whether this is as good as it gets. From a certain point of view (perhaps an occidental economic viewpoint) it would be fantastic if the good people at home didn't care for ethics at all.

I started a business studies course this year, and it was made quite clear that ethics in a business model are both optional and *crippling* to a company. In reality, it may have been different but in the models we were drawing up to adhere to the scheme of work, losing money with touchy-feely humane stuff would be giving your opposition a leg-up.

It *worries* me that what we are being taught does not, perhaps, have ethics in mind. I notice in our society, especially through certain types of media, that wealth is seen as success, second only to 'true love'. People are not encouraged to expect reasonable profit margins. They keep as much money at the top of the chain as they can, instead of feeding it down.

Not everything is taught with an ethical dimension, although certainly everything *has* an ethical side. Whether we choose to ignore it or not – there is a living, breathing world outside of the classroom filled with real people, real concerns and *history* that is the cause of what you are studying. Hopefully you will find real application back in the world once you are done with learning it.

We are born in a world of ethics, so to be without ethics while teaching seems to be taking a step back from the application of the subject. But, because the subjects are teaching us about real people and real works (sooner or later most things are history), it might not be what we set out to discover that brings the ethical aspect.

While studying *Frankenstein* for my English GCSE we had some quite interesting thoughts – not just from the obvious issues tackled within the novel but also in the history behind it. Mary Shelley's father William Godwin believed in philosophical anarchy, where the only laws that needed to exist were those that stopped people from harming one another.

I talked with the people in my immediate area. What about the environment? This seems to leave people free to harm the forests and the seas. If they are harmed, this eventually indirectly harms everything. Deforestation doesn't 'harm anyone', for example, but an eventual lack of oxygen might. Where do we draw the line?

This idea, perhaps, is explored in Mary Shelley's Victor Frankenstein – he did no *harm* to anyone, and his work was intended to help. But his work ended up, through bad parenting, being destructive. What an interesting point! What a good thing to put in our essay! What if that discussion was open to everyone? Who else may have benefited?

Discussion is so often hushed away and frowned upon in class – perhaps not because the thoughts are unwelcome but because of time constraints within the lesson. Teachers have to hold a tight ship.

In my school, regular enquiries are held in Belief, Philosophy and Ethics (like religious education but meatier) – and I find them immensely useful as a means to explore any subject. Suddenly, instead of teaching involving a unidirectional flow of knowledge, it becomes a communal space for all in the room. Even the quietest, those who wouldn't want to stop the class to ask a question, are able and enabled to speak.

Our beliefs about what is real and otherwise directly influence how we interpret what is being taught. If you mention God in a modern science lesson more often than not you'd be told to keep your imaginary friend to yourself. But in an enquiry situation such ideas are much more welcomed. And people from all kinds of the spectrum of belief may open up and share.

It's not something that comes up in casual conversation but something many people can benefit from in a bit of depth. The ethics of education are all around us – in the people we know and the things that we see – but bringing that into the classroom needs openness. Everything we do in our sealed classroom bubble has a very real counterpart in the outside world.

I think that a community of philosophical enquiry opens up an almost humanist approach to these ideas by engaging people and making them think 'What if this happened to *me*?' As petty as this might sound, such subjects stop being so distant and I have seen people apply their own knowledge much more in such a situation, drawing on anecdotes from people they know and giving their own opinion on matters.

Since when have people's opinions mattered in the classroom? If anything, the curriculum tries to keep them firmly out of the way. This sharing session allows our ideas to be considered instead of being hidden away. Surely our opinions on the world directly influence how we interpret questions?

If people disagree with you – then maybe you should review your opinion or maybe you should openly defend it. I think that it can be helpful to make people engage with and openly think about these ideas in ways that might not be how the curriculum intended them to be applied. (Genetically engineering plants to be more hardy? Won't that upset the balance? Is it worth sending us into uncharted environmental waters?) It both opens it up to a human, moral side and a way of tying in facts with real situations and new applications. It allows us, perhaps, to make connections within our minds to see how such information affects us. And even the most stunted in terms of empathy can see the ethical issues when they apply to them. When in an enquiry someone pipes up and goes, 'But that's not very fair, really, is it?' I smile because they have clicked. Something that may have seemed distant to them before has become something they can relate to.

In an enquiry you are asked what you think and feel and are allowed to expand in whichever direction you would like to explore. There is always a human aspect: biological ethics; all manner of global effects and concerns in human geography; history offers insight into what happens today, while maths and physics are just ways of explaining what we find around ourselves.

It is possible that some people do not immediately understand how things that are taught tie into what it means for them. (China's economy? But I'm not in China. Deportation of a man? I am not that man.) One of the best ways is to allow the people you are with to help apply their own knowledge to the matter at hand. It is probable that people in a group *will* care, but for different reasons. Would we have found the connection without this discussion? Quite possibly not.

But morals exist. It's about giving them the floor and letting people understand. A group of 30 in such a scenario will not only learn together but will teach each other. We are studying for exams that don't necessarily have space for ethics, in a world that doesn't necessarily care about them. Surely, it is *necessary* to facilitate in every person who passes through a schooling system the means with which to think about such issues, even if only the seeds of the means. Surely an open-minded debate* with people of varying views, to whom you might not otherwise talk, is the first step to educating young people to manage life effectively and humanely in an ever-changing world. Because a solution that is not humane is … a problem.

*I read somewhere that the Wright brothers would periodically switch sides during an argument, so they could impartialize themselves and get a better assessment of the situation, *and therefore* make better conclusions.

I do not actually know if this is true, or where I heard it – but even if the citation is false what it *says* is interesting.

Appendices

Appendix 1: Cognitive 'habit' checklist

This checklist corresponds to the ten cognitive 'habits' that are looked for in the community of enquiry (discussed in Chapter 6 and mentioned in Chapter 8). The first list can form the basis of an observation sheet or the basis of a teacher evaluation of either an individual student or of the whole group. The second version is adapted for students to evaluate their own or a friend's work in the community of enquiry.

Individual or group evaluation

	YES	NO	MORE OR LESS
1. Makes relevant questions 2. Constructs with and builds on the ideas of others 3. Accepts reasonable criticism 4. Is willing to listen to others' points of view 5. Respects others and their rights 6. Backs up opinions with good reasons 7. Gives examples and counter-examples 8. Tries to uncover underlying assumptions 9. Makes balanced evaluative judgements 10. Addresses comments to others in the class and not just to the teacher			

Individual evaluation

	YES	NO	MORE OR LESS
1. Can I form relevant questions? 2. Can I build on the ideas of others? 3. Can I accept it when others disagree with me? 4. Am I willing to listen to other people's points of view? 5. Do I show that I really respect others and their rights? 6. Can I back up my opinions with good reasons? 7. Do I know how to give examples and counter-examples? 8. Do I try to uncover underlying assumptions? 9. Can I make balanced judgements based on evidence? 10. Do I make sure that I address my contributions to the whole community and not just to the teacher?			

Appendix 2: Thinking skills that are developed through the work of the community of philosophical enquiry

REASONING	ENQUIRY	CONCEPT FORMATION	TRANSLATION TRANSFERENCE
Connecting two ideas together logically	Forming hypotheses	Making distinctions	Listening
Making inferences	Offering examples and counter-examples	Noticing subtle differences between ideas	Sensitivity to others' feelings
Giving good reasons	Questioning appropriately	Detecting similarities	Inferring and appreciating others' world view
Making good analogies	Contrasting	Establishing connections	Empathy
Detecting underlying assumptions	Asking for evidence	Reasonableness	Having an open mind
Thinking hypothetically	Demanding criteria		Respect for others
Syllogistic reasoning	Being sensitive to context		Dialogue
Detecting contradictions	Self-correcting		Putting your ego in perspective
Standarization	Creating alternatives		Self-control
			Following the enquiry where it leads (not just remaining aware of one's own concerns)
			Being aware of the well-being of others

Appendix 3: GCSE Religious studies scheme of work: Religion and Science

A model for embedding the community of philosophical enquiry into a scheme of work linking with thinking skills and concept formation.

Year 9 GCSE topic: Religion and Science
By the end of this unit:

All students   will be able to describe religious ideas about the origins of the world and of humanity

will be able to describe scientific ideas about the origins of the world and of humanity

will be able to describe religious ideas about the purpose of humanity

will be able to describe the relationship between people and the rest of the planet – environmental issues.

Most students   will understand that Christian and Hindu beliefs about the origins of the world and of humanity influence their actions in their lives

will understand that scientific beliefs about the origins of the world and of humanity influence many people's lives

will understand that Christian and Hindu beliefs about the purpose of humanity influence the way they live their lives

will understand that Christian and Hindu beliefs about the relationship between people and the rest of the planet influence their response to global environmental problems.

Some students   will be able to synthesize and evaluate clearly, with reasons supported with evidence from others' experience, Christian and Hindu beliefs about the origins of the world and of humanity

will be able to analyse, synthesize and evaluate the claims of Christians and Hindus about the purpose of humanity

will be able to interpret the evidence, analyse, synthesize and evaluate different beliefs that Christians and Hindus have about the relationship between people and the rest of the planet.

Lesson	Key words, concepts, skills, attitudes	Intended learning outcomes AT1 and AT2	Methods, resources and homework K/V/A	Cross-curricular Links: literacy/maths/citizenship/PSHE	Assessment National Curriculum level
1	Analysis (thinking skill) Empathy (thinking skill) Fairness (thinking skill) Respect (thinking skill)	**Lesson title: An introduction to the GCSE and the course** **All students** will understand they are beginning the GCSE. **Most students** explore reasons why they will find this course useful in their lives. **Some students** will be able to compare different reasons why this course is valuable and to weigh up carefully the best reasons.	**Hand out new textbook** **No homework**	Citizenship: Raising awareness that different viewpoints exist about the origin of the universe. Literacy ICT	N/A
2	Big Bang (concept) Cosmology (concept) Enquiry (thinking skill) Reflection (thinking skill) Evaluation (thinking skill)	**Lesson title: Scientific views about the origin of the universe** **All students** will learn more about the scientific views of the origin of the universe. **All students** will have the opportunity to reflect and generate philosophical questions for an enquiry next week. **Most students** will be able to differentiate the best questions for the enquiry. **Most students** will complete a thoughtful piece of work about their own views on the beginning of the universe. **Some students** will be able to develop more advanced thinking about the origin of the universe following reflection of the experiment from the particle accelerator.	Students watch short You Tube clip about the particle accelerator. Discuss with teacher and develop questions for enquiry next lesson. Draw a picture or write a poem about their views about how the universe began. **Homework:** research regarding the work of physics and the particle accelerator.	Citizenship: Exploring difference Literacy: ICT: research homework	

3	Self-understanding (thinking skill) Enquiry (thinking skill) Reflection (thinking skill) Evaluation (thinking skill)	**Lesson title: Enquiry on the scientific views of the origin of the universe** **All students** will be able to develop a first hypothesis about the chosen question by writing in books 'At the beginning of this enquiry I think ... because ...'. **Most students** will contribute orally to the enquiry individually or in small groups. **Most students** will be able to *understand* what took place in the enquiry to help them make *progress* with their thinking about the question by writing, 'At the end of this enquiry I think ... because ... A contribution that helped my thinking was ... because ...'. **Some students** will be able to analyse moves made in the enquiry that allowed for progression with the question.	**Community of philosophical enquiry.** (A/K) **Desks arranged** so the group sits in a circle. **Select a question for enquiry.** **Students building on skills developed in term 1** **Experienced teacher carefully facilitates the enquiry encouraging students to** ***build on each other's ideas.*** **Homework:** students develop written piece at home showing their understanding of the development of their thinking about the question. Writing frame available.	Citizenship: exploring difference, developing cultural literacy	Teacher observes development of listening in teacher–class enquiry notebook. Teacher observation of student participation. With Year 9 use student evaluation of enquiry using the 'myself as a thinker' sheet.
4	Evolution (concept) Natural selection (concept) *The Origin of the Species* (key text) Darwin (key name) Investigation (thinking skill) Expression (functional literacy skill)	**Lesson title: scientific views about the origin of humanity** **All students** will develop their understanding of the theories of Darwin. **Most students** will appreciate the consequences of Darwin's theory when considering the purpose of humanity. **Most students** will be able to give good reasons for their views about evolution. **Some students** will recognize the	Starter: define key concepts. Students reflect upon how the concepts will raise questions and problems and also influence the way someone lives their life. Think ... DISCUSSION POINT	ECM (meaning . student well-being) Literacy showing good reasoning.	The responses to the discussion questions will reveal development on the levels for RE.

#	Concepts / Skills	Learning objectives	Activities	Links	Assessment
		consequences of the theory of evolution for questions about the purpose of individual lives.	'Has science explained everything?' 'Are there any questions remaining now?' (Follow up and link with their research from the previous lesson.)		Assessment of the will include formative/ diagnostic marking to support each student's progress through the levels.
5	God (concept) Creation (concept) Beauty (concept) Purpose (concept) Mystery (concept) Reflection (thinking skill) Open-mindedness (thinking skill) Appreciation and wonder (thinking Skill) Investigation (thinking skill)	**Lesson title: Christian views about the origin of the universe** **All students** will understand that there are two creation stories in the Bible. **All students** will learn and appreciate the first creation story. **Most students** will understand the first creation story is not a literal explanation but was written more as a song of praise. **Most students** will understand that this is a very ancient story. **Some students** will be able to develop a reasoned opinion building on the views of the scientists.	Read the first creation story together. Explanation from teacher about the antiquity of this story and to cosmo-vision of the Hebrew people at this time. Students draw the story in their books.	Citizenship links : different cultural stories of the origin of humanity ICT: research using internet	Teacher supporting each student's learning according to the GCSE grade anticipated. Teacher monitoring standard of response to the challenging questions coming from this lesson.

6	Creation (concept) Morality (concept) Innocence (concept) Responsibility (concept) Analysis (thinking skill) Respect (thinking skill) Application (thinking skill)	**Lesson title: Genesis 2–3** **All students** will understand that there are more than one creation stories in the Bible **All students** will draw a representation of the Genesis 2–3 story on a double page. Right-hand side reflecting on the situation before the 'fall'. Left-hand reflecting on the situation after the fall. **Most students** will be able to appreciate and make an informed judgement about whether life was better before or after the fall. Which would they prefer: innocence or knowledge? Moral knowledge? **Some students** will be able to develop an advanced reasoned argument about which existence would be preferable.	Read the stories in Genesis 2–3 Double-page spread. Left side: the situation on the garden before the Fall Right side: the situation in the garden after the fall. **Homework:** Development of an argument regarding which would be preferable: to live in the garden before or after the fall? I think …. Because …. However, someone else may say … … In conclusion …	ICT. Citizenship: ECM: moral responsibility well-being	Homework marked according to agreed guidelines.
7	Authority (concept) The Bible (key text) Old Testament (key text) New Testament (key text) Gospels (key text) Revelation (key text) Interpretation (thinking skills) Open-mindedness (thinking skill) Appreciation and wonder (thinking skill)	**Lesson title: Writing a GCSE exam question** **Everyone** will learn what is required in two parts of a GCSE question. **Most students** will be able to write a good GCSE answer. **Some students** will be able to write an outstanding answer.	GCSE questions have different parts. In this lesson students will learn how to write knowledge and understanding responses to trigger questions. 'Describe Christian teachings about the origin of the universe and humanity'	ICT Citizenship ECM	Teacher assessment will be based upon GCSE marking criteria.

		Lesson title: Hindu ideas about the origin of the universe		ICT: Use of Internet/Cleo Website.	Assessment: Consideration of the way students respond to the written/drawing task and
8	Reincarnation (concept) karma (concept) Respect for all (thinking skill) Evaluation (thinking skill) Interpretation (thinking skill)	**Lesson title: Hindu ideas about the origin of the universe** **All students** will learn about the various Hindu ideas about the origin of the universe. **Most students** will appreciate that Hindu ideas and scientific ideas are not in conflict with each other. **Some students** will be able to develop a clear argument about the possible conflict between religion and science (or otherwise).	Introduce Hindu idea of time (cyclical). Introduce new key words: karma and reincarnation. Teach the story of Purusha. Students draw the cosmic man in their books. **Home work:** to complete the drawing of Purusha.	ICT: Use of Internet/Cleo Website. Citizenship: global awareness	Assessment: Consideration of the way students respond to the written/drawing task and Differentiation supported and guided by the teacher and observed through student response to this task.
9	Worship (concept) Prayer (concept) Expression (functional literacy skill) Evaluation (thinking skill) Respect for all (thinking skill) Open-mindedness (thinking skill)	**Lesson title: Thinking Hats lesson 'Religion and science do not mix'** **All students** will be able to realize that the answer to the trigger question will be complex. **Most students** will be able to develop a good GCSE-style answer to this question and complete for homework **Some students** will be able to write an advanced and extended response to this trigger question.	Thinking Hats lesson. Question: Religion and science do not mix See examination board website for details. **Homework:** write *detailed* evaluation question in response to the trigger question. Use the material from the Thinking Hats lesson to inform their answer.	Citizenship: learning about concepts that have greatly influenced the development of values predominant in the UK.	Homework: assessed according to GCSE criteria.

		Lesson title and objectives	Activities	Cross-curricular links	Assessment
10	Stewardship (concept) Environment (concept) Sustainability (concept) Understanding (thinking skill) Expression (functional literacy skill) Respect for all (thinking skill) Open-mindedness (thinking skill)	**Lesson title: Christian ideas about stewardship** **All students** will learn the meaning of the key word stewardship in the context of Christians' views about their responsibilities to the environment. **Most students** will be able to recognize the kinds of actions that a Christian will make as a consequence of her beliefs. **Some students** will be able to develop a reasoned argument about how human beings should behave in relation to the earth.	Mind-map (teach introduction to this properly … trunks and branches …) environmental problems facing the world today. Introduce the key word 'stewardship. Explain with examples.' Introduce the key concept sustainability. Discuss its meaning. Write definition. **Homework:** Research different organizations which help to care for the earth and advance education about these things.	Literacy: this assignment is designed as a literacy related assignment developing writing skills appropriate for religious education.	The assessment piece will be marked diagnostically and according to department mark scheme for this assessment piece.
11	Understanding (thinking skill) Environment (concept) Sustainability (concept) Stewardship (concept)	**Lesson title: understanding how beliefs influence actions** **All students** will be able to develop their skills in writing a GCSE answer. Students will be able to recall from Year 7 work that beliefs influence actions. **Most students** will be able to write a good response. **Some students** will understand and be able to evaluate the best options about working for sustainability. They will be able to develop a considered opinion about whether having a religious background would help develop more sustainable action in the world.	Share findings of the homework … which organizations are working for sustainability and environmental care? Teach about the aim of a B part answer. Model an answer. Students write reasons (unaided) to the following question: 'Explain why a Christian might choose to work for an environmental organization.'	Citizenship sustainability ICT research Literacy	Assessment piece marked according to GCSE criteria. Level given.

12	Mystery (concept) Science (concept) Religion (concept) Enquiry (thinking skill) Investigation (thinking skill)	**Lesson title: Developing philosophical questions about the work of the course.** **All students** will have the opportunity to reflect and generate philosophical questions for an enquiry next week. **Most students** will be able to differentiate the best questions for the enquiry. **Most students** reflect deeply about the complexity of views which exist on the topic of the universe. **Some students** will be able to develop more advanced thinking about the origin of the universe following reflection on the experiment from the particle accelerator.	Use the resources from the whole term's work with the students to develop philosophical questions that enable a deepening understanding of the complexity of the questions. Students to appreciate the significance of the implications of the consequences of the answers to these questions in terms of human responsibility and changes in behaviour needed.	ICT: research the question for homework to support the enquiry next lesson.
13	Self-understanding (thinking skill) Enquiry (thinking skill) Reflection (thinking skill) Evaluation (thinking skill)	**Lesson title: Enquiry on the origin and purpose of humanity and the universe** **All students** will be able to develop a first hypothesis about the chosen question by writing in books, 'At the beginning of this enquiry I think … because …' **Most students** will contribute orally to the enquiry individually or in small groups. **Most students** will be able to *understand* what took place in the enquiry to help them make *progress* with their thinking about the question by writing, 'At the end of this enquiry I think … because … A contribution that helped my thinking was … because …' **Some students** will be able to analyse moves made in the enquiry that allowed for progression with the question.	**Community of philosophical enquiry.** (A/K) **Desks arranged** so the group sits in a circle. **Select a question for enquiry.** **Students building on skills developed in term 1.** **Experienced teacher carefully facilitates the enquiry encouraging students to** *build on each other's ideas.* **Homework:** students develop written piece at home showing their understanding of the development of their thinking about the question. Writing frame available.	Citizenship: exploring difference, developing cultural literacy.	Teacher observes development of listening in teacher–class enquiry notebook. Teacher observation of student participation. With Year 9 use student evaluation of enquiry with the 'myself as a thinker' sheet.

References

Ausubel, D. P., J. D. Novak and H. Hanesian (1978), *Educational Psychology: A Cognitive View*. New York: Holt, Rinehart & Winston.

Arendt, H. (1977), *Between Past and Future*. Enlarged edn. New York: Penguin.

Balchin, T., B. Hymer and D.J. Matthews (eds) (2008), *The Routledge International Companion to Gifted Education*. London: Routledge.

Berlin, I. (1996), 'On Good Political Judgment', *New York Review of Books*, 43.15 (October).

Chambliss, J.J. (1996) *Philosophy of Education: An Encyclopaedia*. New York: Garland.

Children's Society (2009) *A Good Childhood: Searching for Values in a Competitive Age*. London: Penguin.

Claxton, G. (1997a), *Hare Brain. Tortoise Mind*. London: Fourth Estate.

— (1997b) *Wise Up*. London: Bloomsbury.

Claxton, G. and S. Meadows (2008), 'Brightening Up: How Children Learn to Be Gifted', in T. Balchin, B. Hymer and D. J. Matthews (eds), *The Routledge International Companion to Gifted Education*. London: Routledge.

Daniel, M., P. Doudin and F. Pons (2006), 'Children's Representation of Violence: Impact of Cognitive stimulation of a Philosophic Nature', *Journal of Peace Education*, 3.2: 209–4.

Department for Education and Skills (2003), *The Sustainable Development Action Plan for Education and Skills*. Norwich: DES.

Department for Children, Schools and Families (2008), *Sustainable Schools: A Brief Introduction*. Norwich: DCSF.

Dewey, J. (1916), *Democracy and Education. An Introduction to the Philosophy of Education*. New York: Free Press.

Diamond, J. (2005), *Collapse. How Societies Choose to Fail or Survive*. London: Penguin.

Disch, L. J. (1994), *Hannah Arendt and the Limits of Philosophy*. Ithaca, NY: Cornell University Press.

Echeverria, E. (2004), *Filosofía para niños*. Mexico City: Aula Nueba.

Erikson, E. (1968), *Identity, Youth and Crisis*. New York: W. W. Norton.

Fesmire, S. (2003), *John Dewey and Moral Imagination*. Bloomington, IW: Indiana University Press.

Gardener, H. (2007), *Five Minds for the Future*. Boston, MA: Harvard Business School Press.

Goodman, N. (1978), *Ways of World-Making*. Indianapolis, IW: Hackett.

Guyver, R. (2008) 'Philosophy and Traditions of Enquiry in the Great History Debate', *The Philosopher*, 56.2.

Hannam, D. (2001), *A Pilot Study to Evaluate the Impact of the Student Participation: Aspects of the Citizenship Order on Standards of Education in Secondary Schools: Report to the DEE*. London: CSV.

Hopkins, R. (2008), *The Transition Handbook. From Oil Dependency to Local Resilience*. Totnes: Green Books.

Ishii, A. (2008), *Youth Advisory Groups – New Allies in the World Bank's Work*. New York: The World Bank.

Kelly, G. A. (1955), *The Psychology of Personal Constructs, Vols 1 and 2*. New York: Norton.

Layard, R. and J. Dunn (2009), *A Good Childhood: Searching for Values in a Competitive Age*. London: Children's Society/Penguin.

Leitch, S. (2006), Prosperity for All in the Global Economy – World-Class Skills. Final report. Norwich: HMSO.

Lipman, M. (1988), *Philosophy Goes to School*. Philadelphia, PA: Temple University Press.

— (2003), *Thinking in Education*. Cambridge: Cambridge University Press.

Marcia, J. E. (1980), 'Identity in Adolescence', in J. Adelson (ed.), *Handbook of Adolescent Psychology*. New York: John Wiley, pp. 159–87.

Mead, M. (2001), *Coming of Age in Samoa*. New York: HarperCollins.

Nussbaum, M. (1992), *Love's Knowledge*, Oxford: Oxford University Press.

— (1995), *Poetic Justice: The Literary Imagination and Public Life*. Boston, MA: Beacon Press.

Overton, W. F. (1990), *Reasoning, Necessity and Logic: Developmental Perspectives*. Hillsdale, NJ: Lawrence Erlbaum.

Peirce, C. S. (1931–58) *Collected Papers of Charles Sanders Peirce*, 8 vols, ed. C. Hartshorne, P. Weiss and A. Burks. Cambridge, MA: Harvard University Press.

Sachs, J. D. (2007), Reith Lectures. London: BBC.

— (2009i) Sustainable Development: Paying for what Government Schoold Do. *Scientific American* May.

— (2009ii), 'Stemming the Water Wars', *Guardian*, 26 April.

Singer, P. (2009), *The Life You Can Save.* New York: Random House.

Solzhenitsyn, A. I. (1975), *Warning to the Western World.* London: The Bodley Head.

Stern, N. (2006), *Stern Review Report on the Economics of Climate Change.* Cambridge: Cambridge University Press.

Sukarieh, M. and S. Tannock (2008), 'In the Best Interests of Youth or Neoliberalism? The World Bank and the New Global Youth Empowerment Project', *Journal of Youth Studies*, 11.3: 301–12.

UNESCO (2007), Asia–Pacific Guidelines for the Development of National ESD Indicators. Bangkok: UNESCO.

UNICEF (2007), *Child Poverty in Perspective: An Overview of Child Well-being in Rich Countries.* Florence: Tipografia Giuntina.

Williams, S. and R. Wergerif (2006), *Radical Encouragement: Creating Cultures for Learning.* Birmingham: Imaginative Minds.

World Bank (2002), *Globalization, Growth and Poverty: Building an Inclusive World Economy.* New York: Oxford University Press/World Bank.

— (2006), *World Development Report 2007: Development and the Next Generation.* Washington, DC: World Bank.

Young-Bruehl, Elizabeth (l994), *Global Cultures: A Transnational Short Fiction Reader.* New Haven, CT: Wesleyan University Press.

— (2004), *Hannah Arendt: For Love of the World.* New Haven, CT: Yale University Press.

— (2006), *Why Arendt Matters.* New Haven: Yale University Press,

Further reading and links

Arendt, H. (1958), *The Human Condition*. Chicago, IL: University of Chicago Press.

Baggini, J. (2002), *Making Sense: Philosophy Behind the Headlines*. Oxford: Oxford University Press.

— (2005), *The Pig that Wants to be Eaten: and other Thought Experiments*. London: Granta.

Benhabib, S. (1987), 'The Generalized and the Concrete Other', in S. Benhabib and D. Cornell (eds), *Feminism as Critique*. Minneapolis, MN: University of Minnesota Press.

— (1992), *Situating the Self*. New York: Routledge.

Benjamin, W. (1969), *Illuminations*, ed. Hannah Arendt, trans. Harry Zohn. New York: Shocken Books.

Biesta, Gert J. J. (2006), *Beyond Learning: Democratic Education for a Human Future*. Boulder, CO: Paradigm.

Cam, P. (1995), *Thinking Together: Philosophical Enquiry for the Classroom*. Sydney: Primary English Teaching Association/Hale & Iremonger.

Daniels, H. (ed.) (2005), *An Introduction to Vygotsky* (2nd edn). London: Routledge.

Deutsch, E. (2000), *Creative Being: The Crafting of Person and Global Philosophy*. Manoa, HI: University of Hawaii Press.

Elgin, C. (1998), *The Philosophy of Nelson Goodman*. New York: Garland.

— (1999), *Considered Judgment*. Princeton, NJ: Princeton, University Press.

Falzon, C. (2002), *Philosophy Goes to the Movies: An Introduction to Philosophy*. London: Routledge.

Fisher, R. (1995), *Teaching Children to Learn*. London: Stanley Thomas.

— (2003), *Teaching Thinking: Philosophical Enquiry in the Classroom*. London: Continuum.

— (2005), *Teaching Children to Think*. Cheltenham: Nelson, Thornes.

Gardner, H. (2006), *Five Minds for the Future*. Cambridge, MA: Harvard Business School Publishing.

Haynes, J. (2002), *Children as Philosophers: Learning through Enquiry and Dialogue in the Primary Classroom*. London: Routledge Falmer.

Law, S. (2000), *The Philosophy Files*. London: Orion Children's Paperbacks.

— (2003), *The Philosophy Gym: Twenty-five Short Adventures in Thinking*. London: Review.

Levinson, N. (2001), 'The Paradox of Natality: Touching in the Midst of Belatedness', in G. Mordechai (ed.), *Hannah Arendt and Education: Renewing Our Common World*. Boulder, CO: Westview Press.

Smith, S. (2001), 'Education for Judgment: An Arendtian Oxymoron?', in Gordon Mordechai (ed.), *Hannah Arendt and Education: Renewing Our Common World*. Boulder, CO: Westview Press.

Splitter, L. and A. Sharp (1995), *Teaching for Better Thinking: The Classroom Community of Inquiry*. Melbourne: ACER.

Sutcliffe, R. and S. Williams (2001), *The Philosophy Club*. Reigate: Dialogueworks.

Other useful links

DfSC Sustainable Schools Strategy: http://www.teachernet.gov.uk/sustainable schools/upload/Sustainable_Schools_doorways.pdf.

DSCF Social and Emotional Aspects of Learning: Improving Behaviour Improving Learning: http://nationalstrategies.standards.dcsf.gov.uk/primary/publications/banda/seal/

UNESCO Intersectoral Strategy on Philosophy. (2006) UNESCO Paris http://unesdoc.unesco.org/images/0014/001452/145270e.pdf

Links to other organizations

Antidote: An organization seeking to advance emotional literacy in schools: http://www.antidote.org.uk/index.html.

The British Council. School Partnerships and the DCSF Global Gateway. http://www.britishcouncil.org/learning-ie-school-partnerships http://www.globalgateway.org The British Council offers support and funding for teachers wanting to develop a global dimension in their classroom. The school linking project described in this book was supported in the early years by a Reciprocal Teacher Exchange Award followed by a DFID Global School Partnerships Curriculum Project grant. This work led towards the DCSF International School Award.

Filosofía para el Cambio/Philosophy for Change
(www.philosophyforchange.org)
is a voluntary organisation existing in Mexico and UK with the aim of promoting and investigating the potential of Philosophical Enquiry with young people in education for peace, justice and sustainability. Philosophy for Change promotes an annual Youth Congress in Chiapas Mexico; bringing together young people from UK, Mexico and other Central American and European countries to learn and equire about these topics in various locations.

The Institute for the Advancement of Philosophy for Children (IAPC)
http://cehs.montclair.edu/academic/iapc/
The IAPC as Institute for the Advancement of Philosophy for Children, was founded by Matthew Lipman in New Jersey. Recognized by the American Philosophical Association for excellence and innovation, it provides curriculum materials for engaging young people (pre-school through to high school) in philosophical enquiry and provides teacher preparation in the pedagogy of the classroom community of enquiry. The IAPC conducts philosophical and empirical research in teaching pre-college philosophy and the uses of philosophy for educational objectives including critical and creative thinking, social democracy and ethical judgements.

The IAPC publishes the novels and teacher manuals as envisaged in the original programme of Philosophy for Children devised by Matthew Lipman, Ann Sharp and others.

Dolls' Hospital – for 3 to 6-year-olds
Elfie for 6–7 year olds
Kio and Gus for 7–9 year olds
Dixie – for 9–10 year olds
Harry Stottlemeyer – for 10–13 year olds (intro to general philosophy)
Lisa – for 13–15 year olds (Ethics)
Mark – for 13–15 year olds (political philosophy)

The Society for the Advancement of Philosophical Enquiry and Reflection in Education (SAPERE) http://sapere.org.uk/
The society was set up in 1992 following interest aroused by the BBC television documentary *Socrates for Six Year Olds*. This hour-long film focused on the work of

Professor Matthew Lipman and his associates (including Catherine McCall) in New Jersey who, over the past 25 years, had developed a curriculum for 5 to 16-year-olds known as philosophy for children. It seeks to build on Lipman's work and promote his approach and other approaches to developing better reasoning, more reflective consideration of values and the development of communities of enquiry at all levels of education and in a wide variety of contexts.

Centro Latinoamericano de Filosofia para Ninos (CELAFIN)
http://www.pijyotan.org/celafin/
Established by Eugenio Echeverria in 1993, CELAFIN supports the training of teachers in Mexico and many other countries of Latin America. It is responsible for translating and publishing the Lipman novels in Spanish in Mexico and they are used throughout the Latin American world.

The International Council for Philosophical Inquiry with Children (ICPIC)
http://www.icpic.org/
Coordinates activities internationally and runs a biannual conference held in a different nation each time.

Index